THE TAO OF TANGO

by

Johanna Siegmann

Canadian Cataloguing in Publication Data

Siegmann, Johanna.
The tao of tango

ISBN 1-55212-410-X

1. Self-realization. I. Title.
BF637.S4S538 2000   158.1   C00-910680-4

TRAFFORD

This book was published *on-demand* in cooperation with Trafford Publishing.
On-demand publishing is a unique process and service of making a book available for retail sale to the public taking advantage of on-demand manufacturing and Internet marketing.
On-demand publishing includes promotions, retail sales, manufacturing, order fulfilment, accounting and collecting royalties on behalf of the author.

Suite 6E, 2333 Government St., Victoria, B.C. V8T 4P4, CANADA
Phone   250-383-6864   Toll-free   1-888-232-4444 (Canada & US)
Fax   250-383-6804   E-mail   sales@trafford.com
Web site   www.trafford.com   TRAFFORD PUBLISHING IS A DIVISION OF TRAFFORD HOLDINGS LTD.
Trafford Catalogue #00-0074   www.trafford.com/robots/00-0074.html

10   9   8

THE TAO OF TANGO

Taoism – or "Tao" – is an Eastern philosophy which acknowledges the harmony of opposites which exist in the Universe. The yin-yang symbol is the embodiment of these opposites: the passive, female yin and the active, male yang.

When these opposite forces are in balance, they unite to form a complete, harmonious whole. Without both forces, there can be no whole.

Even in men and women.

Table of Contents

Beyond the Dance Floor

Finding Your Balance

THE TAO OF TANGO

Preface

I have often been described as outgoing, aggressive, impulsive, intimidating, gregarious, courageous, and daring. Masculine energy traits. However, I have never been addressed as "sir", or even been described as masculine. In other words, I am feminine physically, with masculine energy. Apparently, this can be very disconcerting to the opposite sex.

Equally disconcerting to women is a man whose female energy is in control, always nurturing, caring and sensitive. What's a woman to do with a man that cries more than she does? And when I look about me, I see legions of people with the same dilemma: physically feminine women with decidedly masculine energy traits, or men who've pounded one too many drums.

Regardless of gender, it seems that too many of us have one thing in common: we are unable to find a mate that matches our needs. We are confused about who or what we're supposed to be, and therefore unhappy.

How often did I hear, "You are so attractive/ funny/interesting/amusing/intelligent, why aren't you with a man?" Yeah?! Why wasn't I? I thought I was doing everything right, even if it didn't feel quite "natural" to my "nature". And I was still the master of failed relationships. On top of it all, I was miserable.

I never believed you needed a partner to be "complete"; a partner should complement you. However, if I have "dominant masculine energy", a "complementary" man for a woman like me would have dominant female energy. Of course, when these men did present themselves, I overwhelmed and overpowered them. I was "intimidating".

On the other hand, I came close to blows with men whose masculine energy obliterated their female energy, since if felt they were trivializing a part of me. I was a "smart-ass" (which is no surprise to my mother…).

We all appeared to be energetically out of synch. What was a girl (or guy) to do?

As a child I was encouraged to follow my dreams, be whatever I wanted, not to ask permission to express my creativity, be my own person, not depend on any*one* or any*thing* for my happiness and fulfillment. I have no regrets about this upbringing, but translating it into a successful relationship had somehow eluded me.

I was alternately described as too independent, too intimidating, too self-sufficient, too aggressive. We were, however, obviously not talking about behavior, because even though I had a really fast sports car and drove like a guy, I was still perceived as feminine.

On the other hand, even though I wore make-up, knew how to boil water, and cried at manipulative movies, men still considered me "intimidating". I just didn't get it.

For years I had been presented with a life lesson that I was simply unable to internalize: the basic dynamics between male/female energies in a committed relationship. Or any male/female relationship. Period.

I was told by those wiser than I that my male/female energies were out of kilter. Heck, if I couldn't even distinguish each in myself (and I was supposedly a quasi-moderately enlightened and pseudo-partially open-minded sort of spiritual individual), how would I ever be able to alter the balance? And a male/female relationship <u>within</u> myself? Was such a thing even possible?

The effort to be more "female/passive" sent me into a panic and left me feeling helpless and stupid. I felt like I had to let myself down, pretending to be weak when I didn't feel that way, compromising my behavior in a way that felt uncomfortable, manipulative, and ultimately, unsustainable. Eventually, I was going to hang the damn picture myself, anyway.

It just never made sense to me, this "female/passive, masculine/aggressive" nonsense. Who decided that women have to be weak and men strong? We each are the way we are. I was born strong. I have big bones...

The notion that this male/female energy was of a more psychic universal nature (and therefore interactive and malleable) and not related to behavior (hanging pictures) was totally lost on me. Like that song in <u>Oklahoma</u> says, "...how can I be what I ain't?"

I couldn't seem to let go of my own definitions:

Female = passive, submissive.
Passive = pushover, pathetic.
Submissive = victim, loser.

I could not make the conscious, spiritual leap
from what passive and submissive on the earth
plane meant when applied to the spiritual,
universal male/female forces.

To realize that both these energies co-existed in
everyone in varying degrees sounded nice in
theory but just wouldn't fit under my skin. I
understood that the balance of these forces was
essential in maintaining any healthy relationship:
with one's partners, work, environment, even
with oneself. But I couldn't imagine how to
achieve this energy balance if it didn't already
exist.

I thought the imbalance was part of the life
lesson, the handicap you had to struggle with
toward "enlightenment". I had no idea how I
could possibly try to be what I wasn't without
losing "myself" in the process. I checked, and
although I discovered a whole bunch of buttons,
none of them said "reset".

"Pretending" to be "feminine" was simply not an
option; not only was it artificial, at some point the
façade was bound to collapse. I simply could not

understand that there was a monumental difference between male and female **_energy_** and male and female **_behavior._**

I had begun to believe that my life was on an unalterable course in terms of my relationships and of my spiritual understanding; of what it meant to be a "modern" woman, caught between the fierce struggle for independence and emotional longing to be cared for; between the outward material trappings of achievement and the intense yearning for spiritual growth. Was I going to have to be "cute" to be loved?

It seemed hopeless. I could not reconcile the theory of male and female "energy" with its practical application. I could not see how I could possibly be both "spiritually balanced" and "materially successful".

Then I received that proverbial phone call that changed everything..

I

The First Step

She: You have to come Tango with us.

Me: Tango? I don't think so.

She: You'll have fun.

Me: Tango? Right...

She: I promise you'll have a great time.

Me: (Groan. Moan. Whine) Fine. But just this once.

Images of Rudolph Valentino lurching across the dance floor with a rose between his teeth played in my mind. Quite frankly, the idea of having strangers pressed tightly up against me in some stiff dramatic mockery of silent movies was just something I had no curiosity about. But I was depressed, coming out of yet another failed relationship, and had promised, just this once, to try it.

I dressed in my most dramatic Tango ensemble (consisting completely of black, of course) and set off, prepared to employ guerrilla tactics on the dance floor if necessary. Instead, I found the Holy Grail.

On a small, uneven-with-a-column-in-the-middle dance floor, in a room with exposed brick walls and red tablecloths with flickering candles in prismed red glass holders, the evening began with a one-hour class to learn the basic step, followed by a *milonga*[1].

Armed with only the bare basic step, I set forth onto the dance floor with anyone who would ask me. Somehow, miraculously, I allowed myself to be led, unconsciously following steps I didn't know I was doing. No one, least of all me, could believe I had never done this before. It had nothing to do with what my feet were doing – what spoke to me was much deeper and far more private and intense.

It overwhelmed and overcame my ignorance of the steps, allowing me to meld with my partner into the dance. I was conversing in some language of the soul that resided in a part of me I

---

[1] Social dance for Tango; also the name of a fast-paced polka-based dance.

never knew existed. I had no way of knowing
that I was consciously experiencing my female
energy for the first time.

In that first hour, I knew my life had changed,
though I could not understand why or how. For
the first time in my life, I felt supremely feminine
yet awesomely powerful, feelings that until that
moment I had never experienced simultaneously.
I was profoundly sensual yet sexually aloof. I
actually experienced the intense joy of being a
woman and never once felt the need to apologize
for it.

Something was definitely afoot, and it was not
just the fancy footwork and the yearning music. I
went home consumed with the desire to relive
those emotions, to live perpetually in that
empowered state, and to find out why this 100-
year old dance had this effect on me.

And from that point forward I became a
certifiable Tangomaniac.

=========

In Life

Preconceived notions can be the death of
personal growth. Had I refused to go dancing

because of what I imagined that dance to be, I would still be tortured with the male/female energy dilemma. With Tango, I experienced a duality —a separation from self which allowed me to experience my male and female energies independently; I was able to observe my own surrender.

It wasn't until a conversation I had with my "guru" that I realized, in one flash of enlightenment, that *Tango represents the very essence of the male and female energies; the dancers are the physical representation of these energies in each of us.* To my amazement, here was the earth plane manifestation of that pesky life lesson! And to my immense joy, it was a lesson I deeply enjoyed practicing.

The dawning realization of this representation struck me like a bolt of lightning. The "I can change a light bulb by myself" side was all ready to fight, but shockingly, the "please tell me what to do" side shut me up. I realized in that one instant that pure female energy was as unrelated to weakness and mascara as pure male energy was to lack of sensitivity and beer belches, that behavior is energy filtered through the ego.

The more I thought about it, and the more I danced it, the more I realized how powerful both energies are. Weakness exists only in the ego's interpretations.

With this new vision burning in my mind, heart and soul, I sought to learn more about it and try to integrate it into my daily life. Now that I had an actual physical and emotional understanding of this "energy" business while dancing (and as a result a new-found respect for each), I was going to try finding it "out there". Life, after all, is a Tango – the male and female energy in each of us engaged in a dance to strike the right balance.

The Lesson

When I'm dancing, everything seems so simple. There are very clear rules, very definite boundaries. During the dance, I feel safe, complete, powerful. When I stop, panic sets in. I fear life encroaching on this safe place. I notice that when I am feeling distracted due to issues in my life, it takes me longer to be comfortable in my dance.

I now see that I carry these petty things with me long after they have occurred. They seem to reside somewhere in my body and are often the cause of my struggle. When I try to dance without clearing my mind, without surrender, my feet are like lumps. They cannot move where I want them to, my legs seem to be attached to another person's body. I get nervous and tense, and my partner can sense it immediately. My upper body gets stiff and I cannot detect his lead.

It is frightening. It depresses me, and this depression makes me mad, all useless emotions in the moment that only aggravate the situation. On days like these, it takes me up to five dances to finally settle down into my body and let go of the chatter in the mind.

I am learning that this "clutter" in life can create needless struggle. Letting go of all of life's little issues as they occur, and getting in touch with the inner basics, is the only way to be free to "dance" — to experience the magical balance of one's own energies. The struggle to get out of my head and into my body goes on constantly when I am not dancing.

To surrender while dancing is easy — I surrender to the external male, the male whose arms I feel around me. But when I am not dancing, I must not only learn to trust the male energy within me, I must maintain the proper energy balance. To surrender while dancing in someone's arms is easy; to surrender while stuck on the freeway is much more challenging.

II

The Dance

I laughed when a teacher told me that in reality, Tango is just walking. Mighty fancy walking, thought I. But when it comes right down to it, Tango is always left, right, left, right, just like walking.

Of course, lot's of complicated stuff happens while you're doing left, right, left, right; there are pivots, and stops, and times when the man is doing one thing and the woman is doing another, but with a different tempo. Just as in life. And the simple act of walking to the rhythm of music while holding each other close is pretty challenging in and of itself.

All of Tango's fancy steps, however, are the artful rearrangement of three basic movements: the basic step, the *ochos*[2], and the *molinete*[3]. Everything else is a derivation/combination of these elements. If Tango is to be symbolic of the

---

[2] Twisting, figure eight steps that require the hips to move while the upper body is stationary.

[3] A turning, "grapevine-like" step that is done standing slightly apart from your partner,

relationship between men and women (and it is), each of these steps is representative of something between the two.

Basic Step – Male and female travel together under the male's lead. To be done right, the female must become one with the male, physically bonded, taking steps of the same length, being in tune with his stops, starts, pauses, bending of the knees, rushing across the floor.

On the other hand, the man must make every move with the woman in mind: he is responsible for her movements. It is this closeness that gives the dances its devastatingly "sexual" reputation. In fact, a great respect for each other is required to do this dance.

"Ochos" – These steps represent the seductive, sensual aspect of the female energy and are almost exclusively done by the female. Even though he leads them, the male must always follow the female as she does them.

When doing the ochos, the woman's feet must always come together, and must brush the floor, always caressing it. This is a very grounding experience. The constant connection with the

floor is very powerful, and completely changes
the experience of the dance.

"Giros/Molinetes" – The man's portion of this
step is called a "giro", the woman's a "molinete".
Of the basic steps, this is the most difficult to
master. It requires the man to spin in place as the
woman moves in a tight circle around him while
they hold each other – sometimes very closely –
her steps helping him pivot around. The closer
the partners embrace the more difficult it is to do.

Depending on his level of skill, a man can do a
giro on both feet, or on one, and do kicks or
swirls with the other. The woman's steps for the
molinete never vary.

Once these three basic steps are mastered, there
are an infinite amount of variations. As one of my
teachers once told me, you never finish learning
Tango (which sounds suspiciously like life…).

There are decorative steps called *firuletes* or
adornos[4], such as *ganchos*[5] and *amagues*[6], which are
very sexy and used sparingly, and step elements

---

[4]A decorative addition to a step, usually a brushing movement, kick, fleck; an
   adornment initiated by the one doing it.
[5]Literally, a hook, where the male leads the woman to kick up her heal between
   his legs.
[6]The opposite of a gancho, the woman crosses her leg over her other knee.

such as *barridas*[7], and *sacadas*[8]. Among one of the more difficult of these are *paradas*[9]. These are difficult to do because it requires complete surrender by the woman in order to feel her partner's lead. If she is propelled in any way by her anticipation, this step can be impossible to do.

Many of the moves are extremely sensual because the feet are always caressing something: the floor; the woman's foot caressing her partner's leg, or vice versa; the woman wrapping her leg around her partner's leg, etc. All these movements, even when done quickly, must be very smoothly.

Tango is very feline in its movements. It is also absolute, which is why it is so dramatic to watch and so fulfilling to do. But in order for Tango to be done well, the male must take complete charge and lead, and the female must completely surrender and follow. Anything less results in a traffic jam.

======

---

[7] When one partner literally "sweeps" their partners foot one way or the other.
[8] Using one's leg to move the partner's leg.
[9] Stops; the male leads the woman to stop mid-step so he may do something else

In Life

I can hear it now - the legions of feminists who
have fought so hard for equal rights with men,
and have, in the process, become "man-like".
Here's where we get screwed up.

> "Why should I always have to follow?"
> "Why can't I lead him?"
> "Why do I have to do that sensual hip
> thing?"

So, why should a man lead and a woman follow?

Because of male and female energy. Because of
universal laws. Because men and women are
different and this is one of the differences.

Why are there traffic laws? We all stop on red
(well, most of us anyway…) and go on green.
Yet no one would argue that they are equally
important for the successful flow of traffic.

According to Lao-tse (the father of Tao), earth
(and everything on it) is ruled by universal laws.
The more we interfere with the natural balance of
these laws, the further we get from the harmony.
The more forcing, the more trouble. Whether
heavy or light, wet or dry, fast or slow, everything

has its own nature already within it. Even men and women.

Leading is male energy; so the male always begins because men have dominant male energy. Following is female energy, so women follow because they have dominant female energy.

Dominant does not mean total or entire. In the context of the natural balance of our energies, it means the major portion. In the context of Tango, it means that once the man leads and the woman follows, the woman must complete the step and the man must wait. The energies are shifted. Doing the step: male energy. Waiting for the step to be complete: female energy. They shift back and forth.

Why is balanced energy necessary in real life? It's what makes for successful relationships, completed projects, a productive working environment, increased communication skills.

If you have weak male energy, you may have trouble making decisions, or focusing. If you have weak female energy, you might leap before you think, always rushing somewhere. We all know someone who rushes in, drops the bomb, then doesn't stick around to deal with the consequences. Or someone who won't stop to ask for directions...Examples of weak female energy seem to be much more plentiful precisely because we are not encouraged to strengthen it.

Tango helps us get balanced because it requires the highest level of communication: without words. It also requires us to use both these energies, and so develops them.

Life in many ways is just like Tango: in order for things to go smoothly, you must use both your male and female energy. In life, as in Tango, you move back and forth between both energies almost unconsciously.

Opposites exist – on every level, in every dimension that we know. Hot and cold. Empty and full. Day and night. Fast and slow. It is absurd to thing of labeling one or the other as good or bad. And yet we readily do so with the terms "male" and "female". I believe we fight against defining our own energies as male and female because one has been glorified at the expense of the other.

Opposites, however, are neither good nor bad – just merely opposite. And we each are comprised of opposing energies - one <u>energy</u> is passive (female) and the other <u>energy</u> is active (male), and to be balanced, everyone must have both. What varies are the proportions. When a woman's masculine energy is in constant control, or a man's female energy is always at the helm, the natural energy balance is altered and confusions arise.

There are always times when a woman's male energy needs to be dominant (at work, in a crisis, divvying up the lunch check), or a man's female energy kicks in (admiring a sunset, a "chick" flick, or the birth of his baby). But for men and women to have harmonious communications, they must always go back to the basic step - the man leads (male energy), the woman follows (female energy).

It is important to understand that I speak of Tango as **an archetypal representation of male and female energy** – I am <u>not</u> suggesting that the behavior <u>during</u> the dance is one that can even be applied our everyday life. In dance there are very clear rules that must be followed in order to succeed. And while there are Universal Laws, in everyday life our energies are subject to a far greater amount of variables.

In Tango, the male is always male, the female, female. A perfect model of each. That is what makes it so much easier to observe – not to mention experience – each energy in its pure state. When you can surrender in a limited, controlled environment, the experience can be much more complete and far less threatening - the perfect learning environment.

The Lesson

I have often been asked why I look angry while dancing. This question always surprises me because, unless I am being kicked, pushed, or stepped on, anger is the farthest emotion from my being. I can see, though, as I observe most other couples, how our expression can be misconstrued.

I believe what is being witnessed is complete absorption - in the music, in the movements, in the joining of two perfect halves– and being totally tuned into each other in a musical give and take, in the perfect balance of male and female.

In the safety of the dance parameters, I can embrace my female energy without fear of judgment, feeling its boundless power; and I can enjoy the male energy of my partner without feeling diminished or compromised in any way.

In Tango, the body position is closely intertwined - partners rarely separate. Like the yin yang symbol, together they create a whole. In Tango, a man's ability to lead and a woman's ability to follow create the whole. Without his ability to lead, no matter how fancy his footwork, the woman will be unable to follow. Without her ability to follow, the woman, for all her poise, will look like she's dancing alone. And yet, once led, the woman must move on her own, the man must wait for her. It is an eternal cycle – the man begins with the lead that the woman follows to the next lead that she follows...

III

The Attitude

I watched the room full of dancers with fascination. They seemed locked into their own little world, some kind of energy transference occurring between each of the couples that swept past me. I couldn't put my finger on it but the women seemed so…womanly, and the men, well… quite manly.

They didn't necessarily look that way off the dance floor, but on the dance floor they were transformed. And this transformation did not just occur between "couples", but between any two dancers. Together they created this sensual third thing. It was almost voyeuristic, watching.

I was both inspired and intimidated. How could I, flunkout of the male/female relationship game, hope to hold my own in such an arena.

Watching more carefully, I could tell the difference between people who were simply doing the steps they had learned or were mimicking other dancers, and those who actually felt what they were doing, surrendering to each other and the music. I was observing the difference between those dancing with each other and those dancing alone.

==========

In Life

The allure (and intimidation) of Tango is its perceived intense sensuality/sexuality. In reality, what we perceive are the male and female energies in action: control and surrender. It is also what makes it so intimidating to those who have watched it.

The steps, no matter how complicated they may seem, can always be learned. But that "sensual" energy that oozes from Tango partners can intimidate even the most self-confident. That sensuality, however, can exist only when the energies are balanced and working together; the freedom to express that sensuality can only exist with each partner's absolute respect for each other.

What became clear to me after my first dance was that the surrender applied exclusively to the dance. As soon as the music stopped, the bodies separated, the air cleared, and that fusion of

male/female, man/woman, was restored to its
separate entities. It was astonishing. It took me
some time to believe that such intimacy could
exist wholly and separately between the dance
floor and the table.

Not that men would not try to connect the two.
After all, men are men (okay…and women are
women). But it was perfectly acceptable, and
expected, that even the most submissive dance
partner was that way only while she danced.

This becomes obvious when you witness people's
personalities return as they leave the dance floor.
Graceful women become strident. Focused men
become timid. After witnessing these
transformations, to say we can't all have balanced
male/female energies is obviously nonsense.

Could it be possible, I wondered, ***that the
same respect and connection could exist
between a man and a woman when they were
not dancing?*** And what was it that connected, if
not their energies? And if it was their energies,
don't these energies exist even when not dancing?

The answer is that the fusion of energies that
occurred only during the dance was possible
because the boundaries during dance are perfectly
delineated and obeyed. If we were able to

maintain those clear boundaries beyond dance, theoretically at least, we would be able to connect the same way in life.

And why not? Isn't life a Tango? And if life is a Tango, then couldn't we expand the balance of energies beyond personal relationships into every other area of our life?

I have had the great fortune of meeting a wonderful man, one whose male/female energies are (in most areas of his life) well balanced. I know, deep in my heart, that we were able to meet because I have also worked on balancing my energies.

The type of people that populate my life has also changed, reflecting my own more balanced energies. Nevertheless, on a day-to-day basis, the practical application of this balancing act is still a challenge, as I suspect it will always be, because our society is not based on the healthy balance of each individual's male and female energies.

I have observed subtle changes in my behavior as a result of which energy I filter it through. In the event of a disagreement in my relationships, pre-Tango behavior would have me attacking the problem head-on, wrestling out an answer when one was not yet forthcoming.

John Gray, in <u>Men are from Mars, Women are
From Venus</u>, explained this concept as the "cave"
and the "wave", which made absolute sense
intellectually. In practice, however, I could never
find the place in myself in which to wait out my
man's "cave" episodes.

In a Tango embrace, these concepts become a
physical experience. Now, when viewed as
expressions of either male or female energies, I
understand these concepts perfectly, and am able
to respect the space he needs to work out the
problem before he can share it with me.

This has all sorts of advantages. By giving him
his space (my female energy "surrendering" to his
male energy), the tension between us lowers, and
we have a chance to actually pinpoint the
problem before discussing it. And instead of
fighting, it really is a discussion.

It still does not feel natural - I will probably
always be of the opinion that it is never too soon
to work out a problem - but it does work.
Further, my respecting his need for space
strengthens my female energy, which in turn
attracts him to me, which in turn.... you get the
picture. The man leads a step that the woman
does while the man waits.

Surprisingly, the more I strengthen my female
energy, the less I <u>need</u> to use my male energy.
When I approach my man as a woman, he does
not feel he needs to compete with me. When he
is not feeling challenged, he feels more
comfortable asking for help – using his female
energy to engage my male energy.

The Lesson

*Sexuality and sensuality are extensions of the male/female
energy balance; sending and receiving male and female
energy in a continuous loop between two people. Sensuality
is pure energy. Sexuality is energy processed through the
body. Sensuality is inner; sexuality is outer. Sensuality is
female energy; sexuality is male energy.*

*Being out of touch with one's dominant energy makes it
difficult to communicate clearly without processing it
through ambiguous physical behavior. Energy is not a
behavior; behavior is ego driven. Our judgment of male
and female energy is in reality a judgment of behavior.*

*Surrender requires trust. Last night I learned something
about trust. Without it, it is impossible to surrender to
your partner. One way of experiencing one's attitude is
through body posture. Until now, I had thought I was
trusting my partner by leaning into him in the correct
posture, yet he kept insisting that I was holding away from
him. Then, while working on a step that required me to*

be leaning completely into him, I realized that he had been right. I had been holding away, not trusting that he would hold me up, not trusting that I would not fall. When I finally surrendered into his hold, the step went perfectly, my legs could stretch out as far as they wanted to and lo and behold, I didn't fall. The absolute energies supported each other perfectly.

IV

The Music

The *bandoneon* is the instrument that embodies the soul of Tango, its very heart. Although it looks like a combination of an accordion and a concertina, its sound is unique. A Tango played without a *bandoneon* has no soul.

Most Tango music is highly complex, especially when compared to other dance rhythms, such as *salsa* or waltz. While the latter have very clear rhythms which dancers must follow, Tango is actually comprised of 2 rhythmically different layers, either of which the leader may choose to follow. He may even change back and forth between either rhythm, or stop altogether.

Generally speaking, there is the bass rhythm, which is expressed by an upright bass or piano, and the melody, which is typically expressed through the *bandoneon* but can also be played by the piano, violin, or a combination.

Many Tangos have an *adagio* portion where there is no bass whatsoever, and the dancing done during this portion is highly interpretive and improvisational. It is also the portion that drives most beginners insane.

There are also different orchestra styles, ranging from highly rhythmic interpretations (such as Troilo), a favorite orchestra for beginners, to very melodic interpretations (Pugliese), a favorite of more advanced dancers. In other words, as in life, there is something for everyone.

The skilled dancer not only has to be in tune with his/her partner, but must listen to the music and obey it. The music has a beat. It has rhythm. And, as in life, it is often very subtle. But it is absolutely there. Like the white line on a road, it is a guide, a basic law that keeps both people traveling together.

If the man does not follow the music, the woman must tune it out completely, since it is not possible to follow both. If the woman does not follow the music, the man is often forced to push and pull his partner.

Either of these events significantly reduces the enjoyment of the dance. Even the most graceful dancers will find it difficult to communicate if they do not follow the music. Without that unspoken communication they will not move as one.

The music of Tango gives the dance purpose, a common language, a path with a common destination. It is the theme, or context, in which this particular communication takes place. With music governing the encounter, everyone knows the rules, and what to expect from each other. Whether leading or following, it is ultimately the music that determines what is done, and how.

Without the music, the steps are only a tug of war between egos. It is probably a good idea to listen to the music even when you're not dancing, until you recognize the rhythm, and can hear it without tightly scrunching up your eyes and getting a headache.

====

In Life

The most common complaint from novices is "where's the beat?" There is no way to convince them that Tango does indeed have a beat - in much the same way as Jazz does. They both improvise above a base line, which requires a different way of listening.

In addition, dancers often subconsciously select an instrument and follow it's rhythm, whether it is the bandoneon, the piano, the bass. Each of these has different rhythms, which is why it is not unusual to see a roomful of couples dancing at different rhythms to the same piece of music. Those with a really good ear can follow different instruments in the same song and therefore move at different speeds, and still be dancing with the music.

In Tango, the music tells you what to do, just as the dialogue in Shakespeare tells the actors what to do. There are very lyric passages, quickly followed by staccato phrases, moments where a lone instrument laments before being engulfed in orchestral sound.

The music is the prevailing theme; it is a story, a relationship. It is evocative, sensual, soul stirring, and playful, each in its own turn. Sometimes it is slow and mournful; sometimes it is purposeful, and yet again it is playful then sensual. And many times all this within the same piece of music. To hear Tango and be unmoved by it is a definite sign that you are removed from your own inner energies.

Life can also be thought of as a series of songs, each with a slightly different tempo, theme, and musical arrangement. And just like Tango, these elements are often very subtle and difficult to hear, especially if you are not paying attention.

Life, like Tango, can be very complicated - there must be a great respect between partners or the dance will not be smooth.

Is the man leading clearly? Does he wait for the woman to finish what he has led? Is he rushing her? Does she know the step? Or is she not listening? Is she anticipating? Can she read his lead? If all conditions seem to be optimal and she still can't, or won't, follow, it is probably because one of you is not following the music.

It is important to take one's time, as with Tango, to discover the natural rhythm that exists in life, and especially between partners. It is there – it can be, and often is, infuriatingly subtle, but once found, it can be the basis for some magnificent improvisations.

The Lesson
Listen. Wait. Carry your own weight.

Until now, I've been worrying that my dance partners might misinterpret my interpretation of the dance. That there would be a tendency to confuse what I was doing in the dance with how I felt about whom I was dancing with.

Last night I had the opposite realization and it opened my eyes to my own insecurities. During one step my partner looked deep into my eyes and I suddenly felt naked and vulnerable. I got embarrassed and realized with a start that I was misinterpreting his interpretation. It was exhilarating, but felt dangerous to me at that moment. It was absolutely like playing with fire in the middle of a drought-ridden field. To submit yet remain apart. To overflow and be contained. Duality.

As I get deeper into the reality of Tango and how it is done when done properly, it seems to be increasingly important to be clear about the dance boundaries. It is extremely important to break that vulnerability that is created during the dance once the music ends.

There is a dangerous line between friendly and too friendly, the latter potentially opening the door to all sorts of confusion, just as it does in life. In my quest for clarity about my outward purpose, I completely forgot about other people's purposes, and my interpretation of them.

It had never been so clear that I have a tendency to fantasy and dramatization as when I am confronted with a partner who is committed to the moment. In that moment, that passion is real; what keeps it from being dangerous and bleeding into reality are the boundaries of the dance itself and the cessation of that connection once we part.

In the process of becoming aware of the moment and practicing being in the moment, the fear eventually subsided, replaced by a longing to be in that place even when not in a Tango embrace, to experience in life that powerful combination of surrender and control without the danger of compromising oneself.

V

The Attire

As frivolous as it may seem, I became
immediately aware of how important the correct
clothing was to this dance. It had to satisfy not
only the sensual aspects of the dance, but it also
had to accommodate its physical needs. For long
steps, a high slit over the thigh; for kicks and
flairs, a skirt that was short enough; for absolutely
everything, a skirt that was long enough...

Watching a room full of dancers, I always became
aware of the clothing only when it wasn't "right".
Any clothing that called attention to itself was not
"right". It pulled focus from the couple, from
the music, from the steps, and prevented the
much sought-after "fusion" of energies.

Any extreme (either male or female) caused both
the wearer and their partner to be preoccupied
with the clothing. Pulling down, covering up,
adjusting, all became additional steps that drew
attention away from their partner.

Unless one is performing in a show, Tango attire
is not "flashy" or "gaudy". It is individualistic,

but not selfish. It is personal, but not self-seeking. It is a way of being yourself, but not at the expense of your partner.

The shoes are also important. In the male, they must allow him to hug the floor and tread on it noiselessly. On the woman, they must do the same, with the exception of high heels.

For me, finding the perfect Tango shoe became the quest for the Holy Grail. Most shoes had soles that were too thick or stiff, making it impossible to feel the floor. Others were too painful.

Complete surrender to the partner is possible only with complete control, something that the wrong shoes – or the wrong clothing – can make impossible. To stop on a dime or turn in place requires a relationship with the floor. If the heels are too high, you are off balance and fall. If the heels are too low, the body position may be difficult to sustain. Sandals don't protect the toes from other dancers. Sling backs allow the heel to slip and you lose control.

If you have to think about your feet for any reason at any time while you're dancing, you're wearing the wrong shoes. If you are able to not think of anything at all when you're dancing, you've mastered the dance.

===

In Life

In life, the right clothing, at first thought, may indeed seem to be a frivolous topic in the grand scheme of life. Yet I remember how I've felt when I've showed up severely under- or over-dressed for an occasion. We are a visual animal. The vast majority of our first impressions are primarily visual. And as a certain shampoo would like you to remember, you never get a second chance at a first impression.

Everything we do, say, and wear, says something about us. Sometimes we think we are sending out one message, but others are receiving a different message. A typical example of this is the extreme sexuality of the clothing today's young girls wear. Not yet knowing what sensuality is really about, they go for the silver bullet - sexuality.

Sexuality is a billboard. Sensuality is the aroma of fresh baked cookies enticing you into the kitchen. To some boys, these girls are saying, "I'm ready", when in reality the girls may only be trying to say, "I'm pretty".

Our judgment of our own energies has made us avoid them by taking shortcuts through behavior.

Tango is often described as sensual, sexual, seductive. So it stands to reason that what you are wearing is an extension of that energy. However, while Tango is sexual and sensual, it is not vulgar. Vulgarity results when the only goal is the end result of appearing sexual. External behavior. Sensuality results when the goal is the process of being connected. Energy.

Tango clothing is the visual manifestation of male/female energy. Vulgarity reflects the behavior, the "dancing by yourself". Sensuality is one half of the whole. Therefore, both the man's and the woman's clothes must enable the dancer to move gracefully. Like the dance itself, the simpler the better.

The more specific your attire, the smaller the circle of people who will feel comfortable with it. It is not only a question of what we see, but of how it makes us feel. What do you feel when you see a young boy in baggy clothes? A woman dressed in a tailored suit? A man in a Hawaiian shirt with plaid pants? A woman in frilly dress, cowboy boots, or leather? A man in a leisure suit, torn jeans, or seersucker?

If anyone of these "outfits" makes you feel at home, and the wearer approachable, then you've found someone you can dance with. The problem is when the message being sent is not the one being received; then you are dancing to different music and someone's going to get his or her shins bruised.

The Lesson

My efforts to balance my energies to their natural proportions have rewarded me with a degree of contentment I have never experienced before. In retrospect, it was this inner struggle that was greatly responsible for the judgment I now am able to observe in so many women: the avoidance of my female energy in order to be "successful."

The development and strengthening of my female energy has resulted in some big surprises. I feel more grounded, more feminine, less strident, and yet am still independent, powerful, and outgoing.

It is only the power source that has shifted, not the intensity of the light. By not empowering half of myself, I was experiencing an energetically anemic life. In demanding respect from others, I lost respect for myself. By empowering my female energy, my ability to pause and

*observe before acting has been strengthened, which in turn
has prevented much frustration, heartache, and
apologizing.*

I have finally been able to create new definitions:

> *Passive = observant*
> *Submissive = centered*

*These and other female energy qualities, though perhaps
not lauded publicly, are appreciated universally. Their
value is the very essence of feminine energy: intimate,
sublime, profound.*

VI

The Body

There is no such thing as the perfect Tango body. Long and lean, tall, short, fat, old, young. It doesn't matter. I recall one of the most sensual dancers I had ever seen. She was doing her "ochos" and the movement of her hips was the embodiment of female sensuality. She weighed at least 200 lbs. One of the men I danced with, who glided across the floor like a hot knife through soft butter, was only 5'6". One of the best Tango partners I ever danced with was a man twice as old as I. A woman in her 80's was ageless on the dance floor.

What each of these people had was the perfect balance of energies while they danced. The women were undeniably female. The men were unquestionably male.

Yet some of the most physically beautiful people on the dance floor looked as awkward as buffaloes in toe shoes because their energies were out of balance. They were doing the steps, and not responding to each other. The women could not be led; the men were unable to lead. Their dancing looked messy, mushy, klutzy. Their physical beauty was obliterated by their inability to relate to each other. However, the beauty that resulted from perfectly balanced energies far outshone any glamour or glitter.

In Tango, we watch the movement of the couple, not the individuals.

=====

In Life

When we witness the perfect balance of energies a paradigm shift often occurs. The woman from who I bought my first pair of Tango shoes told me of her own experience. Several cast members from a Tango show in town came to her store to buy shoes. How could these people call themselves dancers, she thought. They're so old and fat.

Then she went to see the show and what she saw had nothing to do with age or weight. Together each couple created a magic that transcended their physical appearance and took her breath away. What she witnessed was the perfect melding of the male and female energies in each person, and the resulting beauty.

It has been as a result of Tango that I have also
begun to question our obsession with our bodies.
As we move further away from our awareness of
our inner energies, we begin relying more heavily
on physical appearance and external cues from
others for our individuality, our self-worth. And
our definition for beauty gets narrower, more
extreme, and more difficult to achieve.

We are increasingly judging beauty the way
Hollywood views beauty: very young and very
skinny. Women diet away their hips and lose
their breasts in the process, which then need to
be implanted…

And men are no longer exempt from this
judgment: recent studies have shown that they
have **surpassed** women in their preoccupation
over body image.

Men undergo life-threatening, personality-altering
steroid therapies in order to achieve the highly
prized boulder biceps, and thunder thighs of their
wrestler and computer game heroes. We are
literally becoming as plastic as the Barbie or GI
Joe dolls we're trying to emulate.

The bottom, unalterable line, however, is that
girls are shaped differently than boys, because
biologically, we do different things. And

although women can certainly aim for a healthy, fit body, men and women will always be different. To fight that is to fight their very essence.

It is a travesty that women are taught to despise what they are naturally. I believe that this is at least partially why men seem to age so much better than women. Men indulge their male energy, while women fight their female energy. If you spend your life fighting yourself, it's going to show.

The Lesson

As my inner energies strengthen, so does the place from which I observe the world. I am more and more aware of how I operate from a place of judgment in my daily life, succumbing to the appearance of things. I am slowly learning to rely less on what I see and listen to all the other cues.

The temptation to rely on the obvious is extremely powerful. External, physical manifestations are easy guides, since they require virtually no involvement or contact. Sadly, this leads us to interpret bodies and possessions as if they were the people themselves. Our "higher" self is rarely called into action.

To respond. Not to anticipate. It is the golden rule in Tango and it is the rule in life. To be always in the

*moment of what is occurring, to respond to something real,
not imagined. To anticipate is to make assumptions about
something that hasn't happened yet, that may never
happen. Creativity is to respond originally, your own way,
within the boundaries of reality. Without rules or
boundaries, there is chaos. In chaos, there can be no
partnership.*

VII

The Posture

If the woman must follow, then the man must accept responsibility for leading. Therefore, if a woman does not follow a step correctly, it is a commonly accepted convention that it is because the man did not lead it well.

Women who might be tempted to gloat because it's all the man's "fault", should be aware that following also implies a responsibility: listening. Once led, the woman must go (control), not plant herself to be dragged about or pushed around. Once having led, the man must let go (surrender) and let the woman do her part. Only when she has completed the step he has led may he then lead the next step.

The man must also be able to read a woman's level of proficiency and common courtesy dictates that he stay within it. To try making a beginner dance more advanced moves not only makes the woman feel bad, it makes him look bad.

This partnership begins the moment the partners agree to dance together, even before embrace. By choosing each other and accepting each other they have entered into an agreement that is governed by a strict set of rules, including how they hold each other.

In order to create the most favorable conditions for their dance, both must shift their body weight slightly forward towards each other – but not so much as to depend on one another for balance. If either partner remains perfectly upright, or even shifts their weight to their heels, it forces their partner completely off balance in order to compensate. Together they must create a neutral third space for the partnership to exist and flourish.

In the Tango embrace, communication is taking place on many levels. Each person is having their own experience of the music and the other person, and must take these elements into account with each movement. The man must lead with his entire body, shoulders, legs. He uses his arms primarily to stay connected to his partner.

Think of a glass of water: the glass contains the water, but does not restrict or control its movement inside the glass. Any man leading with the arms is exhibiting very poor form and will invariably be pushing and pulling his partner around.

On the other hand, the woman must surrender to the embrace without hanging on to the man. She must neither push off of him nor pull herself to him. Each partner moves on their own axis in an extremely close orbit to each other. When the lead is done correctly, the man creates a space for the woman to flow into.

====

In Life

I have discovered that submission (female energy) has nothing to do with weakness. Even though I surrender to the man's lead, it does not compromise my own integrity.

I could never understand this until I experienced the separation of male/female energy from male/female behavior and understood them as separate concepts. In fact, in order for me to move correctly, I have to maintain my own balance, my own space, my own independence – all expressions of male energy in the woman. To not do so means falling over or tripping on my partner's feet.

In other words, the dance is not only the perfect representation of the male and female energies working together, it is also the experience of both energies within each person. While the female energy is submissive, reactive, and responsive, the male energy is directive, active, dominant. All people need both these energies to function properly.

In the man, the male energy leads. In the woman, the male energy is what keeps her separate from her partner and what she uses to complete the steps. Without it she would lose her mobility and be unable to actualize her creativity.

In the man, the female energy is what keeps him connected to his partner, what allows him to wait for her, and where the imagination for the next step comes from. In the woman, the female energy is what allows her to surrender to her partner, to accept and trust the process of being led. If there is an imbalance of either energy in either partner, he would be unable to lead her, and she would be unable to follow him.

It is the same in life. If both partners try to lead, they run into each other. If both wait to be led, they go nowhere. You must take turns. The cycle begins with the male because male energy leads and (most) men have dominant male energy. This is a universal law, which society (ego) has come to interpret as unfair, an unfairness arising from the judgment that one energy is better than the other. In order to be balanced, this judgment must be surrendered.

It has taken me a long time to implement this rule, especially in my intimate relationships, because come hell or high water, I have always been determined to get to the bottom of an "issue". Out-of-joint-noses were usually the result of these seek-and-solve missions.

By embracing my female energy and thus strengthening it, I give us both the space we each need for the next step - a loving one rather than a pugilistic one.

When giving each other "space", it is important to understand the distinction between turning away in a disgusted "oh-yea-well-forget-about-it" attitude, and one where one's integrity is not compromised. You remain two separate bodies, connected by the music of life, each maintaining their own space, independence, and balance. As in Tango, it is dangerous to become completely dependent on each other for any step in life.

In Tango, there is a style called "*apilado*" in which the male and female lean towards each other dramatically. The partners depend completely on each other to remain standing. If there is any misunderstanding at all, disaster will result, and someone will end up on the floor.

If this were applied to life, we would call this an unhealthy co-dependence. But in a healthy relationship, even if you are closely united by the dance, you must still be able to move independently from each other without causing your partner to collapse.

Because it is a dance, it is only natural that once in a while there will be toes that are stepped on, shins that are kicked. Should this happen, take a step back, work out the scuff, and embrace your partner for the next step. Remember always to lean slightly forward toward your partner – it is how you connect and where communication begins.

I remember the night I performed in front of my peers for the first time. I believed that my years of stage acting would get me through just fine. I was wrong. I experienced fright as I have never had on stage. My innards turned to jelly, my breathing stopped, everything shook. My only conscious decision was to keep breathing. The only thing I had to rely on was total trust in my partner, who'd had over 50 years of experience.

Trust. I didn't realize how enormous that trust had to be. It is the complete and ultimate type of surrender; maximum trust. And although we were highly and enthusiastically praised afterwards, I was aware of my own stiffness and rigidity, two qualities that are anathema to any dance.

What part of me was so terrified? The ego? The possibility of failing? Of being judged by those more experienced than I? Fear of the unknown, fear of allowing the uncontrollable to take control? I had to surrender to that ephemeral creative energy, and I was unable to do so. Although I trusted my partner, I didn't trust myself. In trying to embrace the step (behavior), I let go of the dance (energy).

The Lesson

Instincts reside in a place deep within, out of reach of the external world. Ego interacts with the external world. Our instincts tell us unerringly what is right for us. Our ego reminds us of what society believes is right. Instinct and ego are rarely in agreement. "Getting away with something" does not make it right. Our instincts do not respond to society's opinion; only the ego does, and our instincts are molded by our ego.

Our lesson is to learn to listen to our instincts; our challenge is to tell the difference between our instincts and our ego, and to respond to what we instinctively know to be right. This is the principle of Tao — to surrender to the natural balance of things. When balance is achieved, the boundaries are clear, confusions and misunderstandings subside, communication flourishes.

VIII

The Basic Step

The basic Argentine Tango step is an eight-count step. The partners face each other; the man places his right arm around the middle of her back. The woman places her left arm around her partner's neck. Her right arm and his left are clasped out to the side, with the hands more or less at shoulder level.

Depending on the level of proficiency and the preferred style, the partner's bodies can be as close together as they are comfortable. Although the partners can look over each other's shoulders as in any other dance, unlike any other dance, both can face in the same direction – the woman to the right, the man to the left, cheek to cheek. This too is a matter of preference.

Tango is like walking –left, right, left, right. It is extremely rare – but not unusual – to take two steps with the same foot (left, left or right, right). Sometimes "double stepping" is only an illusion, a syncopated pause while the woman moves before he continues on the same foot.

The man's foot pattern is as follows:

1) right – back
2) left – left
3) right – forward (first brushing past other foot)
4) left – forward
5) right – together
6) left – forward
7) right – right (first brushing past other foot)
8) left – together.

The woman does almost the same thing but backwards. Her foot pattern begins with:

1) left – forward
2) right – left ~~right~~
3) left – back
4) right – back
5) left – back, crossing over right
6) right – back
7) left – left (first brushing past other foot)
8) right – together.

If you still need a picture….His and Her foot diagrams appear on Pages 134 and 135, immediately following the Exercise Section.

The key to dancing Tango is the transfer of weight. Even if it is extremely subtle, it must be absolute. As in walking, even though one's weight is divided between both feet, there is one instant all the weight is transferred from one foot

to the other. It is this weight change which is the
golden key to leading, the first clue that tells a
woman which foot to start on, which direction to
turn.

If the woman cannot feel the weight shift, she
will have a hard time following. If the man
cannot feel the woman shift, he will not know if
she's completed her step and he can continue.
When the weight is constantly divided between
both feet, neither partner will be able to tell what
the other is doing; communication breaks down.[10]

==========

In Life

Everything I have learned about the balance of
male and female energies in oneself begins with
the basic step. Leading and following, the passive
and the active, one's own male and female facets,
are all contained in the embrace of Tango.

When one looks at Tango partners one does not
see either the man or the woman but both
together, equal, united as one. Even when apart
while dancing, it is always the completeness of the

---

[10] Before attempting to do the Basic Step, do the seven exercises found
at the end of this book.

two that one sees. Absolute male and absolute female, separate yet joined, opposite but intertwined, different yet related. The one without the other is inconceivable; it does not exist in Tango.

So it is in life: we cannot exist without this balance and expect to live a harmonious life. At best, we would be dancing by ourselves.

I feel that most of the strife in our lives is as a direct result of judging our energies – a judgment arising from the confusion between energy and behavior. When we judge one energy "better" than the other, we create an ever growing and increasingly destructive energy imbalance.

The most visible effect of this judgment is the need for "anti-discrimination" laws, legally imposed "steps" designed to govern the behaviors and attitudes we have developed towards these energies. Unfortunately, the laws succeed only in underscoring the imbalance, an imbalance which will worsen the more we move away from the "basic step".

Like the basic step, one's energies are the basic building blocks of one's psyche. Why do women consider equality as being equal to men? Why is it that women would spend a day as a man, but men have no interest in spending a day as a woman?

Partly because we have been taught that women (often confused with female energy), are weak and undesirable (except as sexual beings). And because the power of a woman is dismissed as non-existent because by definition, is not obvious. Therefore, the reasoning goes, a woman has no power. And men (not to be confused with male energy) cannot tolerate weakness. Energy is natural and merely exists; behavior is learned and can therefore be changed.

If male energy is to be characterized as movement – generally advancing – there will inevitably come a time when we need to move backward (female energy), or retreat. To judge retreating as "weak" (because it is "female") only serves to limit us, not strengthen us.

As long as we seek a relationship – any positive, nurturing relationship, or wish to interact positively with society – we are going to have to learn the basic step, which cannot be done without female energy.

The Lesson
It is through physicalization that we learn spiritual lessons. Theoretical versus practical. Hypothesis versus

fact. While in the mind, even the craziest theories can be rationalized, worked out, accepted, approved. But the minute we try to put them into practice, it's like working with the image in the mirror – things rarely go the way you imagined they would.

I recall the epiphany I experienced with my very first step. All that fuzzy mumbo-jumbo about male-female, passive/aggressive suddenly crystallized. I <u>knew</u> what it all meant. I <u>felt</u> what it meant. I <u>understood</u> – mind, body, and soul – what it meant. I could see each clearly, independently of each other <u>and</u> their connection. And nothing else I had ever done – no sport, class, art project, spiritual exercise – had even brought me close to this living, breathing knowledge.

The archetypal nature of Tango, with its extreme representations of male and female, was able to bring to the earth plane what before had been concepts floating around in the ether. We as humans have been wired to require physical experience to understand intellectual concepts. No matter how many times you tell a child that fire will burn, "burn" has no meaning until it is experienced physically.

Until you are able to experience the power of both male and female energy in yourself, you will be unable to respect and embrace them both.

Beyond the Dance Floor

IX

The Master

I remember one night, when I first started going
to Tango clubs, watching the swirling bodies of
dancers. Suddenly, I caught a glimpse of
someone who was dancing unlike anyone else in
the room. I couldn't put my finger on it, but this
man's movements were simplicity personified.

He filled every movement of his body, every beat
of music, with intention, emotion, fluidity. He
followed the music. There was an economy of
movement; there was no wasted energy. And
even though his partner was doing steps as fancy
as anyone else, I could not see his lead.

How was he doing that? I looked from him to
every other dancer in the room. They may have
had fancier moves, but he had them all beat.
What exactly was it? There was no hesitation, no
indecision. Purposefulness. He was leading with
no doubt – absolute masculine energy.

To my great surprise and excitement, he asked me
to dance, and I was able to experience first hand
that "invisible" lead. The first realization I had

was that he was following me! I was setting the
pace and level of our dance, and he was
respecting it. As a result, I was able to relax and
follow him in return. Not once did he pull or
push me to where I was "supposed" to be. If I
did not go where normally expected, he would
adjust to me. It was the first time I actually
<u>danced</u>, never once thinking of the steps.

=====

In Life

That very night, after literally taking two steps
with me, he asked me to be his dance partner.
He had recognized my own female energy, even
when I had not. Without my even understanding
it, we had connected in an absolute way, a natural
way.

I had no way of knowing it at the time, but I was
immensely fortunate – he was, and is, an
exceptional dancer. I learned priceless lessons
with regard to the dance, and as a result, to life
itself. He knew the rules of the dance, as any
master would - how to lead, when to wait, the
perfect balance between male and female energy,
which in turn helped me balance my own.

Off the dance floor he was – like most of us - not quite as masterful. It made me realize how difficult putting this male/female energy theory into practice could be. While on the dance floor, the rules are universal, everyone agrees to them, follows them, and life is wonderful. In dance, the rules follow the natural balance (Tao) of the universe.

There are also universal rules in life, but we get very distracted, lazy and seduced by the obvious and no longer obey these rules. When the music stops, it's as if anarchy sets in; the very same rules we all agreed on while dancing send us careening to opposite ends of the boxing ring when the music ends.

To observe the dance floor as the dancers go from dancing to "regular" is a fascinating exercise. Men and women go from flowing to awkward, back to flowing, never even realizing they are doing so. For us to continue to flow with each other, we need to become aware of our energies and how we use them.

The Lesson
I recall during one Tango, my partner and I experienced a sublime moment: I had taken a step he had taught me and done it with real feeling – the first time I had completely

*embraced my female energy. The difference was
astonishing. There was a moment when our eyes met and,
in that instant, I experienced a mixture of fear and power.
I realized why Tango is so powerful.*

*In Tango there is the fear of being totally vulnerable and
the seduction of being in complete control: male and female
energy. To be myself completely with my partner, and trust
that he will understand that it is part of the dance, and not
anything else. To trust that what I do will be interpreted
within the confines of the dance. Then to witness the effect
of what I do on my partner.*

*That is the power. The power to play and then say no.
The power to draw the lines, as if to say, this is everything
I am, and I'm not giving it to you. It is for you to see and
admire. But it is mine. You cannot take it unless I give
it. And the choice is mine. The danger is of course in
using the power to toy with your partner in life.*

*I became aware that the intrigue of Tango social life had
the potential of destroying the magic of Tango. It is the
very nature of the dance that brings out passion in people.
When we discover something valuable we wish to hoard it.
There is a lot of jealousy, bickering, hierarchy. Good
dancers are as much admired as they are reviled.*

*My partner had a terrible reputation for choosing young
partners and then wanting to take it beyond the dance
floor; however, I never experienced him as other than an*

*absolute gentleman. Yet someone was apparently
spreading rumors that he and I were more than a dance
couple. Then I heard that he was the one spreading the
rumors.*

*I started to wonder, too much probably, if I should say
something to him, ride it out, or correct the rumor. He
had told me when we first started dancing together that the
jealousy of others will make them try to tear us apart, and
I began to wonder if the people telling me about the rumors
were in fact making up the fact that there were any.*

*I realized that when I became concerned with these
preoccupations, it interfered with what he and I were doing.
I became inhibited, and worried that I was going too far, of
what others might think was going on between us.*

*It's hard to rationalize that what people say is not as
important as how I feel, and what I know: instinct, energy.
We both knew the truth, and that should have been
enough. As long as he respected my boundaries, there
should really not have been any issue.*

*I realize now that I believed the story (behavior) more than
the reality (energy). The "what if" pulled my focus away
from "what is".*

X

The Power of the Woman

At the risk of making it sound like Tango is the
ultimate male fantasy of bondage and submission,
it is important to note that Tango empowered me
in a way that I have rarely felt. It allows me to be
completely female and totally in control, a state I
rarely experienced in life.

While the man may lead a woman to do the steps
he wants, the woman interprets the step, <u>as long
as she obeys the music</u>. Neither partner, for all
their interpreting, should disobey the music. It is
the foundation upon which the dance is built. In
this context, the woman is in control and the man
must submit to her will, waiting until she has
finished her step.

It may sound contradictory to be both submissive
and in control, especially when describing the
same person, but both these energies exist
simultaneously within each of us. It is both the
male and female energies working symbiotically
which makes this possible.

We do this on a daily basis, in every activity we perform, from simple conversation, to complex activities. Men and women are constantly switching off between our male and female energies, using them alternately as needed in a give-and-take in life, just as we do in dance.

The fear of surrender is a tangible and rational one: allowing someone you don't know to make decisions that involve you is very intimidating. On the other hand, the responsibility of making decisions that involve someone else is at least as intimidating. Until the notion that following can in fact be a powerful experience, neither partner will experience the power of surrender.

In giving up control we actually gain control – as soon as a woman is led, she has the step to herself, to do with as she wishes, and she has a captive audience: her partner. The entire time the woman is completing her step, he must wait and follow her. In waiting we can observe, and enjoy.

====

In Life

In today's world, our society has evolved to the point where a woman must often live her daily life using her male energy to the exclusion of her

female energy. Men are encouraged from all
angles to purge themselves of their "female"
energy. Both men and women suffer an energetic
imbalance as a result of this one-sided
encouragement, which has serious repercussions
on our health, our children, and even our
environment.

If she is employed, a woman must operate with
her male energy almost to the exclusion of her
female energy. Intuition and consideration will
laugh her out the door – she must resort to an
approach that men find comfortable and thus use
her male energy. It is often this energy that labels
women "bossy" (and worse).

To complicate matters, if a woman is in a dating
mode, social protocol almost demands the
"Dutch" approach, unless she is willing to make
other "concessions". So instead of being able to
"switch shoes" into a female role, she is using her
male energy with a male. This only confuses the
male since he is now responding to male energy
in a female form.

Unless he is able and willing to operate primarily
in his female energy, the relationship will fail: you
will either become "pals" (which may be the wish
anyway), or you will enter a relationship that will
end as soon as the energies are re-balanced. Men

are empowered by a sense of control, of being able to lead. To diminish this power by "equalizing" the date upsets the natural balance and the dance comes to an end.

Female energy is not a liability, a weakness, or something to be hidden or make excuses for. We all need to learn to embrace our female energy and be empowered by it, not embarrassed. As long as women feel the need to apologize for being female they will feel compromised, and men will continue to reject their "feminine" side.

But even passivity has boundaries, and those are what we need to make clear - to be a woman does not require an apology, nor does it mean you can be taken advantage of. And although my female energy is passive, it still has boundaries that you must respect, if you want to dance with me.

Over the course of time our faith in female energy has been eroded by the constant demands of the "show me" male energies. Our very society requires that everything we do leave proof of it having been done. This is the only way to reap tangible rewards, which are the only rewards we have come to prize.

Through Tango, the process of learning to trust one's female energy is amplified and accelerated.

Because it is isolated from our male energy we can observe it and experience its power, which is completely different from that of male energy. Bridging that trust into daily life is the lesson.

There is a natural fear or apprehension towards female energy, especially in men. Unlike male energy which is obvious, the nature of female energy is quiet, mysterious, hidden. Perhaps as a result of this subtlety, it is dismissed or ignored. But the dark side of the moon is there even if we can't see it, and it is just as important as the side we do see.

As humans, we fear that which we do not know; by its nature, female energy is not obvious and is therefore unknown or misunderstood. It is this unknown element to which the male barroom behavior is reacting. It is the mystery in each of us, the introspection. It is partly why men reject their own "female" energy. And almost nowhere in our culture are men encouraged to embrace, or even explore, this energy.

As a result, women have begun developing their male energy at the expense of their female energy as a way of maintaining contact with men. The paradox is that no matter how much women behave like men, men will always see them as what they are: women.

The Lesson

In my own search, I kept seeking to be more of something I could not understand. It wasn't until I could recognize that "something" within myself that I was able to strengthen it through observation. Recognizing is the first step toward change and growth. My fear of "losing" a part of myself to something I could not understand or identify with took a very long time to quell.

Through Tango, I found myself in a situation that was non-threatening to my ego, where I could explore that aspect of myself that I knew so little of – female energy. I, like the majority of our society, mistrusted and misunderstood that half of myself, the greater portion of my energetic make up.

Without knowing it, this mistrust was transmitted to every relationship I had ever had; it rendered me unapproachable and intimidating to men, basically because my male energy was dominant. I would attract men physically but – like to magnets of the same polarity – repel them energetically.

I have been applying the lessons of Tango to my life for some time now, and the difference is astonishing. My own inner struggles with my male "gotta-take-care-of-it-myself" energy, and my female "I-will-allow-this-man-to-help-me-(even-if-I-can-do-it-myself)" energy, have subsided to fairly undetectable levels most of the time.

In the most evident development of this balance, I am now blessed with the kind of relationship I had always dreamed about. And he does not even dance Tango!

It took a long time and a lot of honest soul-searching to realize why I felt so compelled to do things myself, and the bottom line was that I had a lack of trust - if you want it done well, do it yourself, is what I learned and believed. This position assumes, of course, that my way is the best, or only, way. If this were the case, I would not need a partner. I could dance by myself.

Through Tango, I experienced the need for trust in order to be a good partner; the more I trusted, the better a partner I became. Off the dance floor, it is much more complicated because there are so many variables, but the rules are essentially the same. By trusting him, I allow my partner to lead. By following his lead, he develops his trust in me. By trusting each other, there can be true communication.

Nothing is more attractive than a man who does not constantly have to prove he is one. In my surrender to him as a woman, he is free to be a man: protective, demonstrative, decisive. In his surrender to me as a man, he is also understanding, caring, and supportive. For a man, this can only happen when there is trust. I have not "lost" a part of myself at all, but have gratefully "found" the whole of me.

XI

The Power of the Man

A gifted dancer will be able to communicate to his partner what his is doing, wordlessly. His clarity of movement and communication makes words superfluous. Gifted couples look like they are one, as though they are reading each other's minds. If he cannot communicate with clarity, they will step all over each other.

I recall one of the very first times I ever Tangoed. My partner was a phenomenal dancer. But as a beginner, I often did not understand his lead. Sometimes he would pause and I would fill that space with some footwork I felt was appropriate. After several such incidents, he looked at me and said

"You are dancing by yourself".

He had, in fact, lead me, and I had not trusted him. I was uncomfortable with the lack of movement when in fact that was exactly what was expected of me. He advised me that if I didn't know what I was meant to do, I should do nothing at all. It was the man's responsibility to let me know what it was he wanted me to do. He was, of course, talking about leading. If I still didn't get it, perhaps he wasn't communicating it clearly enough. It is the man's job to clearly communicate what he wants. Only when he does can everything go smoothly.

A clear lead is often confused with a strong lead. A clear lead can be soft or strong, but it is always clear. A strong lead, on the other hand, can be too strong, and is not always clear. Some of the best dancers seem to have undetectable leads, in terms of touch. And yet, by using their entire body, they are able to communicate the most intricate steps, the quickest change of direction.

On the other hand, an overzealous lead will throw the woman off balance, which in turn throws the man off balance. A too powerful lead is more of a push (or a pull), which compromises the balance between partners because the woman has to compensate, and her compensation will in turn affect the man's balance. Besides, no one enjoys being pushed and pulled around the dance floor.

This man's words made me aware of how much I resisted surrendering to, and trusting, my partner, and that if I "listened" to his lead, I would never again be "dancing by myself".

====

In Life

Male energy is not about men's behavior. Male energy recognizes and thus respects the boundaries of female energy, and a man in touch with his male energy has no need to stampede past those boundaries. Once again, communication is the key: the man may lead the step, but a woman may not follow.

For men, this is a mind-bender. The bull-in-the-china-shop approach to women is still very highly prized between men. And like it or not, most men are more interested in impressing other men than in attracting women. Most men find impressing other men much more motivating (or their ridicule much more intimidating) than the admiration of a woman, no matter how high her heels.

Winning the attention of a woman scores points with other men. Therefore, embracing their own female energy goes against everything they believe in or the image they want to project. Granted, we're talking about your average you-bet-your-butt-I'm-from-Mars male. And "wus-iness" is not a quality they want to cultivate in themselves.

Neither is it a quality women should want to cultivate.

It all boils down to a P.R. problem: female = wuss. As long as women embrace that concept, and feel that way about their female energy, men will certainly not embrace it in themselves.

It is this very rejection of female energy that I believe is at the root of abuse. To reject is not enough; that mysterious quality that cannot be explained or understood must instead be dominated, vanquished.

To suppress his own female energy a man must, by extension, suppress women. Every time that energy makes itself felt, he must suppress it by objectifying it as a woman – a woman that he is able to control.

Tango is once again reflective of life in that most men cannot communicate to their partners what they need (feelings/female energy) without a lot of symbolic pushing and pulling. Most men are even unable to verbalize anything connected with emotions to anyone, least of all to a female.

This is especially true if he is suppressing or completely removed from his female energy. If he is suppressing his female energy it is likely he is unable to make contact with his feelings. On the other hand, too much female energy leaves him unable to take action, lead, make a decision. This leaves his partner confused, frustrated, and if a decision needs to be made, forces her into the male position.

The man's power may seem quite obvious by the very nature of the male energy, which is kinetic, as opposed to a woman's, which is static. But this is not where the man's power lies. The male power lies in the ability to be in complete control and yet remain responsive. To lead; to communicate. It is not so much a matter of bossing around as it is leading. When one is led somewhere, there is eagerness to follow. The reaction to being pushed is to resist.

The Lesson

The biggest lesson of all - trust - is the one that feels most rewarding when learned. Trust is faith in the absence of evidence.

After months of dancing together, weeks of rehearsing, of doubts, of frustration, hope, anger, fear, and disappointment, the day of the big show was finally upon us. To be selected as one of the few from a field of dozens of couples, was in and of itself an honor my ego clung to vigorously. It ran with the importance it bestowed upon this selection and made the rest of me miserable.

Try as I might, the enormity of it engulfed me and suffocated me. It got in the way of my feet, my partner and I, and my life in general. The thought of it filled my every waking minute. And even as I accused my poor partner of dancing by himself in his head while holding me in his arms, I submitted him to the same torture. That he didn't turn on his perfectly polished heels and leave me for good alone with my neurosis was his demonstration of trust, that this too shall pass.

The trust I had been struggling with and which I still had to develop, needed to be strong enough for me to surrender completely. Over the course of those five months, I realized that this process involved surrender of the male energy (control); surrender of mundane problems to the dance (distraction); surrender of attention (allowing someone else to tell me what to do - which alone was a major obstacle).

I needed to transform myself into an empty vessel in order to be transported. I was shown that the fear of surrendering in this manner is due to feelings of inadequacy - mine, his, ours. If I let go, who will catch me; if I empty myself who will fill me - and with what; if I'm not in control, who will be? Trust.

In the process of stumbling toward our mutual trust, I noticed that our dancing suffered various insults.

Depending on who was less trusting at the moment, the steps were alternately jerky, messy, frenzied, and unsynchronized. My challenge was giving my partner the space he needed to learn the choreography, something he had a great deal of trouble with. His challenge was in allowing me to do my part, contribute to the whole.

When we each met our challenge, the dance went smoothly. When we didn't, Band-Aids were required. Our bodies became stiff, we didn't breathe and neither of us went where we were supposed to go. And finally, in the most extreme instances, we resorted to complete male/female stereotype behavior: I would jabber away and he would tune out.

Were it not for our mutual respect for each other, for that higher something that we channeled through the dance, and for the fact that we had come from my very first Tango steps to a commitment that involved others, we might have called it quits.

But something greater was at stake for me: the lessons I had been learning so rapidly about myself through the instrument of Tango might have come to an abrupt end. I felt as though swept up by a monstrous wave that would either drown me or carry me upon its crest to safety.

For weeks, and even in the hours before the show, my chest was constricted by the grip of fear. Breathing, chanting, meditating, push-ups, nothing would loosen the grip. It was not until one hour before the show that I suddenly experienced the surrender. It was in that instant, when I let go of my expectations, my obligations, my fantasies, that I was freed of thought and judgment and allowed myself to be an empty vessel. And I was filled with joy.

I glanced at my partner and we both realized we were in the same place. We had somehow bridged the gap with trust. The energy that was created between us cleared the fog of fear that had enveloped us until then. When we stepped out on stage, we were connected to each other and our bodies responded accordingly.

By any measure, our performance was a success. But for me, the greater reward was having surrendered. It was the tangible benefit I derived from trust. My guru told me to draw the symbol for yin/yang and contemplate it. As I did so I realized that it is also the symbol for Tango which, in and of itself, is symbolic of male/female energy. Two halves caught in a swirling embrace; sensual yet contained, movement with definition. Both halves are identical yet opposite, they are fluid yet have a center, and only together are they a whole. It is the symbol of a complete self. It is the male and female energy in each of us. It is Tango.

XII

The Power of Balance

In a quietly lit room, a sensual swell of music begins to fill the air. Two people look at each other. He extends his hand toward her; she accepts it. He draws her toward him slowly until they face each other closely. In a simultaneous movement, they embrace each other and fuse into the music. Instinctual, natural, they move as one, which in essence they are.

There is no thought concerning who does what or why. It just is. In each other's arms they move, think, and breath as one. They are jointly separate, uniquely united, independently combined, respectfully uninhibited. In this fusion there is still a balance that is essential for its very existence.

A movement begins, flows, and ends, to be followed by another movement which begins, flows and ends, and by another until the music stops. Together they build something greater than who starts and finishes, who leads and who follows. In each other's arms, there is no judgment about being a man or a woman. Within the dance, they cannot exist without each other. Without her, his initiated step wouldn't be completed; without him, her completed step would not be followed by another.

When the music stops, they let go of each other and the myriad of life's variables intrude. The intimacy of completed forces is shattered, and awkwardness sets in.   Judgment.   Regret. Expectation.   Separated from each other, male and female energy face one another, the energies are witnessed.   In each other's arms, within the parameters of the music, the cycle of energy is completed; the energies are experienced.

Off the dance floor, outside the rules of dance, and the guidance of the music, each energy stands alone, unless we create the balance within ourselves.

========

In Life

Advance	*Retreat*
Control	*Adapt*
Definite	*Infinite*
Exclusive	*Inclusive*
Expand	*Contract*
Fact	*Theory*
Individual	*Communal*
Literal	*Figurative*

Logic	*Intuition*
Overt	*Covert*
Physical	*Spiritual*
Public	*Private*
Sex	*Love*

A list of words. Opposites. Just opposite.
Neither one superior nor inferior to the other.
Neither one necessarily describing a man or a
woman, yet both are qualities that exist in both
men and women.

If we were to label one list as left "brain" and the
other right "brain", or outer and inner, there
would probably be no "stigma". The fact that we
now call them male and female may have
something to do with the general qualities of the
sex they're named after.

But, how did one get "better" than the other? Is
one "better" than the other? Why is one
"weaker" than the other? Why is "weak" "bad"?
Why is it that men especially are so adamant
about not having "female" energy? Is an
obedient soldier weak? Is an understanding boss
weak? Depending on the context in which the
energy is expressed, it may be the only proper
expression.

Again, I am only referring to the *energies*.
Behavior is socially influenced and not of a

universal nature. Witness the friendship behaviors of American men versus mid-eastern men. Physical contact between American men is considered extremely abhorrent (even between father and son the only generally acceptable physical contact is a handshake), while mid-eastern men hug and even kiss each other openly in greeting. It is our social interpretation and the expression of our energies that changes, not the energies themselves.

I believe that much of the judgment comes from the very terms "male" and "female", which have sadly come to mean more (or less) than what they are: opposite. On the earth plane we have come to interpret female qualities (even in women) as weak and undesirable, except perhaps in the sexual arena.

When we deride one or the other, we are referring to men and women, not male and female energy. Our society demands that we excel, yet the commonly accepted yardstick by which we measure that success is by and large male. How and why did this come about?

Women have eternally struggled for "equality", a term that has been interpreted to mean various things throughout the ages. Today it means equal to men – something that seems to be universally

interpreted as "the same as" men. Fortunately,
no law can ever make men and women the same.
Nor should it.

Women seem to have gotten caught up in
becoming "the same as men" in every sense,
including energetically, which means they need to
turn away from their female energy to be
successful. Since the female aspect of a woman is
precisely her liability in our society, it is not so
difficult to turn away from it.

However, women who do defend "feminism" are
using their masculine energy to do so and are
therefore considered militant (masculine).
Unless we learn to distinguish the difference
between male and female *energy* and male and
female *behavior*, we will not be able to cultivate an
equal respect for both energies.

Without that respect, equality will always mean
"the same as" men. This is precisely where I was
when I discovered Tango. Through Tango, I was
finally able to distinguish the difference between
male and female energy and behavior.

Why are women so threatened by "men only"
clubs or bars? Although it could be interpreted as
a physical manifestation of men rejecting women,
I don't believe that is why they exist. We all need

places we can go to get away from each other. But places where only men are allowed are threatening to women because they interpret it as a rejection of themselves.

The fact that there are also "women only" places does not make it "equal" because men could care less if they are not allowed into women's places. It is still somehow "inferior" because it is a female place – "male" having a preferential position in our society.

Our society is beginning to witness more and more incidents involving women behaving in increasingly violent behaviors – violent crime, drinking binges, physically abusive "hazing" rituals, to name a few. It is clear that women continue to believe that *behaving* like men is empowering.

In their struggle to be more "equal" to men, women are forsaking the very essence that makes them women, and in so doing, minimizing its position in the universe, and undermining the very importance of its existence.

Because the energies and the behavior are not differentiated, and because women are "inferior", men will never embrace the female energy in themselves. And because in our society women tend to want what men want, they will turn away from themselves.

If we continue down this road, men and women will only differ visually, a process that has already begun as a backlash: women are reclaiming their "womanhood" by adopting extreme sexual attire – even in the workplace.

In an ideal world, men and women would recognize that they compliment each other. That to be complete, balanced, harmonious and happy, each has something that the other needs, and that one does not have to be destroyed for the other to flourish. That the male physical can be tempered by the female spiritual, and the female intuitive can be focused by the male active. One does not destroy the other. One helps the other grow and expand.

Why we have developed such judgment may have something to do with how the male and female energies are interpreted in our society. Male energy is obvious, evident, external, while female energy is subtle, quiet, mysterious. People do not trust what they cannot see, what they cannot understand. What is evident does not need introspection, so it is "easier". What is external does not require self-examination, so it is also "safer".

The ethereal is impossible to prove in earthly
terms, so it involves invoking faith and trust,
characteristics that are not cultivated or popular
in today's society. And because this mysterious
energy is the "female" half of the energy balance,
it is attributed to "women", who are therefore to
be mistrusted and conquered. It is why men fight
so hard against recognizing female energy in
themselves – it is not to be trusted. It belongs in
women, who are not to be trusted.

A muscle can be made, manipulated, exposed.
And it can create immediate, obvious changes
when applied. A thought by itself, though equally
powerful, is internal, not immediate or obvious.
Each is influential in its own way, but humans
have come to trust and prefer speed, efficiency,
and immediacy.

The Lesson

*I watch the ocean from the safety of the shore. The waves
come thundering toward me, pounding on the sand with an
explosion of power. Then, for the briefest of seconds, that
power is suspended between coming and going, before
retreating stealthily into itself. An eternal cycle in a
rhythm that is primal and universal. The roar, the sigh.*

*Who can watch this dance and not recognize the power?
Who can say one is more powerful than the other – the*

*forceful, crushing invasion of the crash and foam, or the
stealthy mysterious retreat into the unknown? The electric,
soul-shaking thunder of surf upon sand, or the soul-
stirring, soothing silence that follows? The deliverance of
the wave or the expectation of the next?*

*Standing in the water, I feel the duality of the ocean's
power. The waves rush in and push me back towards the
shore; as the wave retreats, its unseen power below the
surface pulls me to the sea. The seen and the invisible; the
heard and the silent; the coming and going.*

*For the most part, these forces exist in equal measure, the
tides ebbing and flowing in perfect balance; at times the
ocean is governed by the male energy of storms or the female
energy of stillness.*

*Which is better? It's an absurd question. As we observe
the vastness of the ocean and its power, we cannot conceive
of asking such a question. It is powerful. Period. In its
completeness it is powerful. The ocean is the very essence of
the union of male and female energy, and it is the union
which is most powerful.*

*We ourselves are such an ocean. Male and female energies
are the tides that course through the human body, a
combination of opposing forces of equal power. In men, the
crash of the waves is punctuated by their silent retreat. In
women, the tides are reversed. To resent this is to resent*

the power that put the moon in the night sky and brightens the day with the sun.

Our energies were created as opposite in order to allow them to exist together. To try and separate them is impossible. To attempt to eliminate one or the other is unhealthy. True happiness lies in the mutual embrace of both our energies.

XIII

Looking in the Mirror

"Look at your right foot: it's all twisted."

Sure enough, reflected in the enormous floor-to-ceiling mirror of the dance studio we were in, was my crooked foot for all the world to see. And here I'd thought my partner and I had struck the prefect, flawless pose.

"Your arm is too stiff; your knees are bent, your shoulders are hunched…" and so the assault continued; the image in my head having borne only a scant resemblance to the image everyone else could see. The gifted inner me unfairly chained to this outer klutz.

In the journey from neophyte to "expert" we all progress through numerous stages – self-consciousness, caution, obsession, justification, rationalization, intellectualization, blame, arrogance – until we inevitably consider ourselves ready for the final stage: perfect Tango show dancers.

By the time I reached this stage, I'd stuffed my closet to capacity with Tango-wear. My shoe racks were overflowing with Tango shoes. I owned every Tango CD ever burned and studied with every Tango show star to stop in town long enough to give a class.

I was saturated with technique, inundated with styles, and adorning my steps to the max. It was, in fact, when I believed there is no inner work left to do – or was avoiding it – that I became obsessed with "how I look", and turned my attention outward.

In this stage, I stole furtive glances in those enormous mirrors as I dance by, under the pretence of correcting my flaws, but secretly admiring my own grace, poise, or creativity, and silently criticizing my partner's evident need for more classes.

There was much to admire: the flirty-ness of my skirt, the felinity of my stride, the position of my foot. I experimented with hair styles, hem lengths, and heel heights. Sometimes, I didn't even see my partner, except as something blocking an admiring view of myself. I sneaked peaks at my progress towards perfection, conveniently overlooking any flaws that threatened the inner image of myself.

Until the teacher – or a clearly more advanced
partner – would point them out.

Even then, I continued to avoid looking at my
flaws directly, or I became obsessed and frozen
by them. In either case, I remained a prisoner to
this incomplete inner image, unable or unwilling
to move beyond this or that detail either because
I refused to see it or was consumed by it.

I would dismiss an instructor's general comments
as pertaining to others, since I could not – or
would not – see them in myself. As a result, my
evolution into a truly good dancer came to a
grinding halt. All the technique and classes in the
world did not address the real problem.

What I could not see was that as long as I placed
my attention on the outward image while ignoring
the inner connection, I was only seeing a partial
picture. As long as my partner's image in the
mirror was no more to me than an obstacle to a
view of myself, the picture was not complete.
After all this time, I was once again "dancing by
myself".

Then one day, for whatever number of infinite
reasons, I finally heard my teacher's or partner's
comments and instead of thinking "that isn't me",

I thought "what if that were me?". The once
locked and blockaded door was now ajar.

With that simple shift in attitude – from "not
me" to "what if" - I finally found the courage to
look in the mirror and see the complete picture:
the fabulous posture with the bent knees; the
graceful movements with the floppy feet. I saw
my complete self: both my beauty and my flaws
which, now that they were visible, could be
corrected.

I saw it all, embrace the reality of who, what, and
where I was. And while it wasn't perfect, neither
was it all that bad.

=====

In Life

It is a daily ritual, the look in the mirror. Upon
rising; upon retiring. I wash my face, I brush my
teeth. I apply make-up or fix my hair, or adjust
my skirt, or match my outfit.

On my daily journey through life, I can check out
my reflection in any surface that offers one, and
note how many people are doing the same.

But what am I looking at? And just what do I
see? Am I admiring the glint of my sunglasses
and my newly-bleached teeth? Or am I steeling
myself for a glimpse of a flaw someone's words
brought to my consciousness?

In my progress through those numerous stages of
Tango, I avoided the big picture as avidly as
everyone else did. The reason I could not do this
or the other step was because it had not been lead
properly. Or the lead was too hard. Or my
partner too short. Or the floor was too sticky,
my heels too high. An infinite number of reasons
that had nothing to do with me, and for which I
was therefore not responsible.

It was this attitude that permeated my entire life.
An attitude that placed me on an unchanging
plateau that stretched infinitely into the horizon.
A trap of my own making.

I recall avoiding my own gaze for many, many
years. It was somehow creepy, and this look-alike
stranger returning my stare made me feel very
uncomfortable. There was an aversion, no doubt
fueled by the fear of discovering something
grotesque, to looking into those eyes. Of
catching myself in a lie; or seeing the hypocrite; of
discovering that part of myself for which I
needed to accept responsibility.

The part that was responsible for my own misery.

Because I knew, subconsciously perhaps, that if and when I ever <u>did</u> accept responsibility for myself, I'd have to do something about it, or I would never know peace. I would never be able to dance.

Even knowing that this was what I had to do for anything in my life to change, it took many years to find the courage to do so. And although the fear of looking outweighs anything we might actually see by a thousand fold, I cannot lie. When I finally did summon the courage to face myself for the first time, it was horrible. It was a kick in the stomach that took my breath away. It was painful and shocking and humbling and humiliating. And for an infinitesimal instant which nevertheless seemed like an eternity, all I could see were the flaws. They occupied the entire universe and suffocated me with their enormity. Like tearing off a band-aid, my entire consciousness was reduced to the infinite pain on one inch of skin.

And then there was the miracle: the watering of the eyes subsided and I realized that I was intact, that I was pretty much who I always thought I was – and more – and that I had just gained true, genuine control for the first time in my life.

I no longer had to wonder "why does this happen to me", but could now ask "how can I change this".

The plateau had been traversed. I could now become a better dancer.

The Lesson

Embracing my true self, exactly as it existed, warts and all, required something I was never previously able to do: accept responsibility. To look at whatever awful or hateful thing I saw in myself and recognize it as part of who I am would never have been possible in my unbalanced state. With my passive/female energy in a weakened state, I was unable to contemplate, observe, and witness without judgment, or of accepting responsibility for who I was. Without understanding my active/male energy, I was racing around in avoidance of that responsibility.

As long as I dismissed my "flaws" as genetic, unfair; beyond my control; ethnic; sexist; cosmic; karmic; or hormonal, I would never be able to touch them or transform myself. By allowing my gaze to skip over my true self whenever I looked in the mirror, the illusion would rule me, boundless and inevitable. My flaws would always be a wall I would continue to bump into as long as I refused to see them.

In retrospect, I cannot deny that despite all the benefits of having looked in the mirror, there were times when, like Nemo in The Matrix, I'd wished I'd taken the blue pill and continued in ignorant bliss, rather than having taken the red one and seeing the truth. The truth I saw was intolerance and judgment; laziness and impatience, that I was opinionated and didn't listen – all qualities I despised and readily recognized in others. Witnessing them was excruciating, and almost awful enough to make me start running again. Almost. The idealized image I held of myself was shattered with just one little, honest glance. But that brief peak at the true image that remained held far more promise than my fantasy ever did.

What I did not yet see under it all, however, was fear. Fear is the most supreme obstacle we must overcome. It is the basis of shame, timidity, and cowardice. It is why we assign blame and why we hate. Fear is the fuel of deception, and why we lie, cheat, and reject anything new and ridicule anything different. It is the enemy of creativity, joy, and spontaneity. And why, no matter how horrendous and torturous our lives are, we prefer to stay in the depths of misery rather than face the unknown.

In my own experience, it took a very long time to recognize fear in myself. My fear was of displeasing others, and it was so great that I preferred to endure unhappiness rather than be the cause of it in others. The images of abandonment, fury, and resentment I imagined I would inflict were enough to stifle whatever urge I had to change, *even though change was the only healthy and logical choice for me to make.*

It was not until I finally saw – and acknowledged – that fear, that was I able to begin any sort of true, profound transformation. It took many, many sessions of looking in that mirror to finally see this sneaky trait in myself.

This does not mean the fear is gone, but that in recognizing it I am able to work around it. Nor does it make change easier, but it makes change possible. As long as the reason to stay put was this fear, I would never be able to embrace change. What I discovered, of course, was that for the most part, the actual reactions of others to my changes never measured up to the fiery drama of my imagination.

As each ugly and frightful piece of myself fell into place, I also recognized that they were but tiny details of the greater "me". By owning them, was I able to put them into perspective, devise a plan, and achieve the changes I desired.

The path to personal growth is never-ending, and the process, once begun, is irreversible. Even so, it takes a lot of discipline and courage to continue looking in that mirror. When I become complacent and comfortable in whatever zone I've entered, I invariably run into another glass ceiling of my own making, another wall within myself I did not realize I had erected. It is only by accepting responsibility for that obstacle that I can begin the process of overcoming it. And every wall I bring down reveals ever greater vistas and grander panoramas of life's beauty.

In the final paradox, I almost relish finding these obstacles in myself, since recognizing them, embracing them, and eventually overcoming them brings me ever closer to that balance and harmony we all seek. In accepting my own flaws and the responsibility for my own mistakes, my happiness is no longer at the mercy of someone else. True freedom of self requires personal responsibility, which is the challenge. But the rewards thus far would make me choose the red pill every time.

Finding Your Balance

Exercises

To begin developing our awareness, we must first develop and strengthen our center. Only from this neutral place can we truly observe and learn about ourselves and the world around us.

Passive energy is critical in developing and maintaining this center, and the following exercises are designed to help you recognize and develop your passive energy, and learn how to use it constructively in combination with your active energy.

Think of any object with mechanical movement, such as a car, or a bicycle. In order to change gears, you must go through neutral. You cannot go from 1st to 4th or from 3rd to 1st without passing through neutral.

In Tango, the more skill you have at finding "neutral", the easier and faster it is to change directions. The ease with which you are able to change directions (without losing your balance, of course), will determine the complexity and interaction with your partner, and the level of communication you will achieve.

It is the same with human consciousness. You cannot learn something new, hear a different opinion, or change your mind if you are unable to let go of one "gear" and listen in "neutral".

Too often we believe we are listening, when in fact we are just waiting for our turn to expose our point of view. Under those circumstances, it becomes a veritable struggle to have a difference of opinion with anyone.

What follows are simple exercises designed to help you develop an awareness of both energies and experience each separately. The first three exercises are done by yourself, and the rest require a partner. There is no right or wrong way of doing them – the process of learning and doing is, in fact, an application of male and female energy.

Since these exercises require both energies, doing them will help you balance them. Focus on the subtle, inner changes (energy), not the feet or the steps (behavior). As you become more aware of the differences between each energy, you will be able to see the opposites in every aspect of your life.

Although these exercises are derived from Tango, eventually any activity you do can be an exercise for balancing your energies, because just about everything we do in life has an active and a passive phase.

As a general rule, I recommend you play music (I prefer Tango, but it's not a requirement) in the background, so that you have an external input for rhythm. This is especially true for the partner exercises. The music will be the external third element (the "theme", see Chapter IV – The Music) which you both must obey. This will help you avoid the "you're wrong/I'm right" obstacle we all come upon when learning something new.

If this is the first time you are doing these exercises, I suggest that you do them in the order provided. Each exercises is built upon the lessons learned from the preceding ones, and are the building blocks towards greater active and passive energy self-awareness.

It is also why the first few exercises are done without a partner; it is simply not possible to become aware of others when we remain unaware of ourselves.

Most of the exercises are also extremely subtle, as is passive energy itself. If the subtleties are lost on you, don't get frustrated, or despair; realize that this a gauge of the relative strength of your energies. Be patient (yet another manifestation of passive energy), and you will one day suddenly become aware of being aware.

Once you are familiar with the exercises, however, you can concentrate on those you feel best address your particular needs.

Exercise #1
Finding Neutral

This exercise is designed to strengthen your observation skills (and thus your passive energy) by focusing on extremely subtle details within yourself. The fact that we predominantly focus our attention outward is the primary reason behind the current epidemic of weak passive energy.

In the stillness of standing, we can turn our attention to extremely subtle changes in ourselves, which would otherwise be lost in the distractions of movement.

Stand with your feet comfortably apart, approximately shoulder width, with your weight evenly distributed between both feet.

In Tango, this is called the "neutral" position because from it you can go in any direction very easily. Close your eyes. Many people feel as though they will lose their balance when they do so. This simply means that you rely almost exclusively on visual cues for your balance. This is also your first indication of your energetic imbalance.

If you simply cannot stand comfortably with your eyes closed, choose a fixed spot about 6 feet from you near the ground and allow your vision to become relaxed and unfocused. With a little practice, you will soon be able to keep your balance with your eyes closed.

First, focus on the physical (active energy) aspect of yourself. Hot or cold? Check your posture. Are you slouching? Are your knees locked? Are you holding your shoulders tightly under your ears? As you do this mental check, try adjusting and relaxing each part that's tight and unbalanced.

Now focus attention inward to the emotional/mental (passive energy) aspect. Are you tired? Distracted? Where are you holding the stress of the day? In this case, simply observe as you take inventory of your inner self.

Before we add anything further, turn your attention to your feet. What is their natural position? Are they turned in or out, or perfectly parallel? There is no right or wrong answer here! This is simply an observation exercise.

What part of the foot are you standing on? The heel or ball of the foot? On the outer or inner edges? Do you have more weight on one or the other? Try shifting around until you find the place where the weight is perfectly distributed in the center of both feet. Take your time. Oh, and don't forget to breathe!

For the next portion of this exercise, you may open your eyes. Shift your weight *very slightly* backwards onto both your heels, being careful not to lose your balance. Notice what happens to your perception of the room.

Now shift *very slightly* forward onto your toes, without losing your balance. Do you notice a difference? Simply observe. Repeat as needed, very slowly. If you move too quickly, you will be unable to notice the subtleties.

As you do these shifts (backwards, forwards, and neutral), try to notice which positions makes you feel more removed, detached, or involved and connected? Is there an emotional response? Is it different in each position? Do you feel weaker or more powerful in any one position?

Do not despair if you do not "feel" anything right away. We are talking about very subtle changes. Learning how to perceive them is the most important step, and you must learn it before you can proceed any further.

If you are like most people, you will find that the slightly forward body position is the most comfortable and most empowering. In terms of communication, it is also very important for several reasons: it shows your partner that you are interested in them and available for communication; it is physically supportive of your partner, and it provides the most control of your body.

Exercise #2
Walking

This exercise is designed to strengthen the connection between the mind and the body.

Not many people are consciously aware of their body, which may sound absurd considering so many people are obsessed with their bodies. But that obsession is with its outer appearance, not its inner workings, its rhythms, its balance.

Disciplines such as meditation and yoga use breathing and heartbeats as focus points. Exercise #1 introduced you to the process of inner awareness. This exercise adds the external element of movement and is designed to help bridge the awareness gap between our active and passive energies.

The most basic activity of our daily lives is walking – yet most of us are unaware of our posture, our breathing, or any other aspect of walking except it's not nearly fast enough when we're late...

If we are to be in touch with anyone else, we must first be in touch with ourselves.

Start by walking around the room. Just your
average, everyday walking. Once you get past the
self-consciousness, turn your attention inward. It
helps if you try to sense your heart beat, or notice
how you are breathing. Then begin paying closer
attention to your posture, your body position.
Where your feet touch the ground. Slow down
the pace if you can't tell. Do this with both feet
and notice if it's the same place or a different spot
on each foot.

Now vary your walk slightly by leaning forward as
you walk. Speed up and slow down. How does
this affect your balance? Does it affect your
stress level?

Adjust you posture in the opposite direction and
lean backwards slightly as you continue to walk
forward. In what way, if any, does this posture
difference make you feel? Which makes you feel
more stable, which less?

As you walk, notice how your weight shifts from
one foot to the other. Do your feet roll to the
outside or the inside? Does one but not the
other? Try to determine the exact place in your
stride where all your weight is on one foot, and
then lift the other. Do you lose your balance?
Try to determine the exact place this happens.

Turn and walk backwards. Start slowly – most people feel very awkward walking backwards since we hardly ever have to do it in our daily lives. As an exercise, however, it is very valuable, is the opposite of forward, and offers its own lessons on awareness.

Eventually work up to the same pace as when you were walking forward. What happens if you lean back into your walk? Or lean forward? Notice the difference.

Walking is nothing but transfer of weight from one foot to the other. Becoming aware of this weight shift is the secret to communicating effectively. It is how you know whose "turn" it is.

The Importance of the Weight Transfer

There is only one place in your stride where your entire weight is on one foot: right in the middle when the feet pass each other. The way you tell if your complete weight is transferred is that you can lift the other foot without falling.

This neutral center is important because it is where the weight transfer occurs, and becoming aware of the weight transfer is the first step toward awareness of our own and our partner's energies.

Slow down your walking and observe it very closely. Become aware of the changes in your balance as you work through your stride.

Continue to ask yourself questions as you walk: are you tense? Where are you holding the tension? How does it affect your stride? When you focus on one thing do you lose focus on something else? When you start thinking does it affect the tempo of your pace?

As you start building the connection between the inner and outer awareness of yourself, you can perform this exercise absolutely anywhere. No one will even know you are doing an exercise!

Try shifting your awareness back and forth from inner (breathing, heart rate) to outer (traffic, temperature). Try any variation of this exercise that comes to your mind. The goal is to increase the strength of both your passive (observation) and active (movement) energies, and our ability to use both with ease.

Exercise #3
The Weight Shift

This exercise builds upon what you have learned in Exercises 1 and 2, and is designed to help you detect the physical weight shift. As your ability to detect this shift sharpens, it will help you detect emotional "weight shifts" in others.

Begin by standing with your feet as close as comfortably possible without losing your balance. Make sure your weight is equally distributed on both feet.

Now, shift all your weight onto one foot. To check if you have done so, lift the other foot about two inches off the floor. Repeat with the opposite foot. Continue to do this slowly until you are able to shift and lift without wobbling.

Now take a tiny step to the side, shifting your weight completely in that one movement. As you step into your center, you should be able to lift the opposite foot off the ground, setting it down next to the other. Do this back and forth until you are able to step directly onto one foot and lift the other without wobbling. Always make sure you come back to "neutral".

It might take time to find your balance, so be patient. As you become more confident, increase the length of your side step; the longer the stride, the more important it is that you bring both feet together at the end.

Now do the same but going forward and backward. Take a tiny step forward onto your "center", lifting the other foot slightly off the floor to make sure all your weight is transferred. As with the side to side steps above, make sure to bring the feet together at the end of the step.

Now take a tiny step backward. It's the backward step which confounds most people. I find it quite revealing, actually, since stepping backwards is the physical equivalent of passive energy, and "letting go".

It might be helpful if you keep your weight slightly forward (as in the walking exercise above) even when stepping backwards. However you decide to try, make sure to start slowly and work up to a consistent rhythm. The object is not to do it fast, but to find your center on each foot, even in the longer steps.

Once you've become comfortable both side to side and back to front, mix them up: step side to front to back to side, etc. Always alternate feet (left, right) and always make sure you finish in neutral by bringing your feet together.

Why is this weight transfer so important? It is where all change of direction – emotional, physical, mental – takes place. It is a point of reference both partners can perceive. It is both the beginning and the end of every interaction. The more complex the movements between two people, the clearer the intentions need to be. And the faster the movements, the subtler the transfer becomes. In order to detect even the most subtle transfers, or shifts, the more in tune you must be.

Since clarity is the most important quality of successful communication, it is important to develop our perception of even the subtlest transfer. Left and right. Back and forth. Whatever direction you go in, you must go through center first.

Do not allow this exercise to be come a "rote" movement. Truly observe and sense the change. What foot are you most comfortable on? On which leg are you least balanced? The more you look, the more you will notice. As your observation skills increase, you will be amazed at how much more you will notice "out there".

Exercise #4
Weight Shift with Partner

Finally! A partner!!! You will finally get to test everything that you have learned thus far on someone else! See if you are able to both communicate your intentions to your partner and perceive their "answer".

This exercise is extremely important as the first step in becoming aware of the "outside world" by focusing outside yourself and on your partner's weight transfer. This is why it was so important to work on yourself first.

In Tango, a man cannot lead the next step until his partner has finish her step, and the only way he knows she's finished is that she transfers her weight.

Injuries can and do occur because a man leads a woman into a step before she has completely shifted her weight from one foot to the other. And a woman may not know what foot to be on because she has not felt her partner shift his weight.

In life, this translates to misunderstandings that occur because of our inability to perceive a change in direction or tone in our partners.

In addition, the inner work done previously improves your sense of balance, allowing for complicating changes and movements without throwing your partner off balance.

If the weight shift is an extremely subtle movement in oneself, imagine the sort of focus required to detect it in your partner. This is why it is terribly confounding to most people. But with proper practice and focus, the weight shift becomes clear as day.

This is also true in communication. One does not start talking until the other person finishes, and vice-versa – you give a signal you're done which allows the other person to speak. These signals may be verbal or tonal "weight shifts", but can also be physical by using body language. If we are not paying attention to each other, these cues can be missed (or are intentionally ignored), and an argument can arise.

Begin by putting on some music. Refer back to Chapter 4 - The Music as to why this is important. I prefer Tango for this exercise because it has a variable rhythm. Music such as swing, or rock have beats that are too regular, and it is easy to fall into auto pilot.

Stand slightly apart from your partner facing each other, and hold each other's shoulders. This is called the "practice position". Determine who will lead first.

Both of you close your eyes. If you are leading, place all of their weight on one foot; if you are following, shift your weight to the same foot. Taking a very tiny step to the side (an inch or two), shift all your weight to the other foot. Do this back and forth slowly, from one foot to the other, making sure your partner shifts with you.

The "follower" should be focusing on feeling this weight shift. Start making the transitions from one foot to the other smaller, until you are doing them without moving your feet at all, shifting only from the hips. Remember to keep your eyes closed.

If your partner is following you closely, you may speed up a little; however, never lose the clarity of the shift – you must shift completely, no matter how subtle the shift. And use the music. Find the rhythm – whether it's that of the piano, the violins, the bandoneon, or the bass – because this will give the partnership a theme within which to work.

Switch roles and do this exercise again. It is very important for both partners to recognize the weight shift.

Now that you have added a partner, it is very easy – and natural – to get frustrated, because you are having to incorporate another person's perceptions and experiences into your own. When this happens, it's usually because the follower is not really following and/or the person leading is not really leading. Rather than assign blame, shift roles and start again, or stop and take a break.

To increase the level of difficulty slightly, do this exercise in the Tango embrace.

Exercise #5
Partner Lead/Follow

The purpose of this exercise is to develop the ability to communicate on a much deeper level. This is the first step toward being able to move together, beyond the weight shift.

As you develop your skills to "hear" your partner's unspoken cues through this exercise, you will become aware of equally subtle cues that exist in every human interaction in our lives.

Do this exercise to music. Stand in the "practice position" discussed in the previous exercise, and begin by warming warm up, using the shifting exercises you did in Exercise #3. Make sure the leader initiates all the movements. Once you have become "synchronized" with each other, it's time to take a step.

The most common problem when leaders first start waling is that they lean away from their partner, afraid they might step on their feet. **It is this leaning away that is going to cause all your problems**. Maintain your upper body "frame", and don't back off. Walk purposefully "into" your partner. Your presence will "lead" them to take a step back, with your left foot replacing the space occupied by their right, and your right taking the space occupied by the left as you walk.

Start with one small step at a time, and come to neutral each time.   Everyone always feels awkward because it feels they have someone else in their way.   If you waiver, the follower will sense the uncertainty, making it even more difficult to lead.

Now take a step backwards.   This will undoubtedly be extremely awkward, for both the leader and the follower. We are simply not used to walking backwards, and we are especially not used to taking a step backwards with someone in tow.   The secret is to remember to keep your upper body position firm, and your hands on each other's shoulders in a firm but comfortable grip. Do not lock your elbows!

If you lose contact with each other, always return to neutral to reconnect. Bend your knees slightly and try again, one step at a time.

Remember that this is a collaboration.   The follower should not anticipate any step, nor should the leader assume that the follower will move out of the way. The leader must lead the step, and the follower must follow the lead. Period.

Whatever you do, DO NOT LOOK AT YOUR FEET!!! It is helpful if the follower closes their eyes. **This will be the first time the follower comes face to face with their lack of trust**. You will tighten up, you will lean back, you will do all sorts of things that will make it quite difficult for you to follow – or even perceive – the lead. This is natural, and it will eventually pass if you continue to work at it.

It is important that the person leading realizes how difficult this moment is for their partner. This is also a good time to show some compassion, since they will be experiencing the same moment when it's their turn to follow.

As this exercise becomes less awkward, you can increase the length of the step. Eventually you will be able to do this with ease.

Use the music as a guide to your movements and don't forget to pay attention to the lead/follow aspect of the movements. The follower may start only when their partner starts.

Now it's time to switch roles, and the leader must now follow. This is an equal opportunity exercise because it is important for both partners to experience the follow (surrender) of female energy, and the lead (control) of male energy.

The concepts of "leading" and "following" are the same whether the leader or the follower is a man or a woman, and whether you are dancing or at a business meeting. Our mental expectations and fantasies about these two energies are rarely the same as the reality. The biggest surprise for both partners is how different either energy is from how we imagined they would be.

Exercise #6
Walk Lead/Follow

This is an extension of the previous exercise. In the practice position, holding each other's shoulders, start walking back and forth. Once again, the choose who leads first. You can walk any number of steps; you can even stop for as long as you want, as long as you lead your partner AND follow the music. If you get the hang of it and want to be really adventurous, you can go to the side, and back. Your body position (chests slightly shifted towards each other, even when walking backwards) will help you connect with each.

The purpose of this exercise is to further strengthen the control (male)/surrender (female) responses. Because the follower does not know what direction the next step will be, complete surrender to the lead is necessary or there'll be a lot of bumping into each other.

It is not unusual for this exercise to begin as a tug-of-war... Start slowly, and if frustrations gets the better of you, let go of each other (or hug...), take a deep breath and start all over again.

Now switch positions. By doing so, both
partners will gain a deeper understanding of their
opposite energies, and thus a greater respect for
them and for each other.

It is equally important for both partners to learn
surrender (follow) as it is for them to learn
control (lead). Any feelings of resentment about
surrender are directly related to a lack of trust.

Exercice #7
Embrace Shift

This exercise is very helpful in increasing awareness of your partner's body position and weight change. In life, it gives us increased awareness of subtle changes in situations and moods.

Recall the body positions of Exercise No. 2 – back, neutral, forward. Now, turn, face your partner, and embrace, remaining in neutral. Focus on each other, then turn your attention inward. How does this position feel? Neutral? Slightly distant? Focus on the subtle energy changes as you work.

Now *leader only*, shift your weight back, follower remaining in neutral. What does that do to the relationship of the embrace? The follower probably feels like they're being pulled off balance, unsupported, like you could fall? Leader, do you feel that your partner got "grabby"?

Shift back to neutral.

Now the *followers only* shift back, leaders remaining in neutral. Notice how this makes you feel about yourself, about your partner.

Back to neutral.

Now both of you shift back. Better? This probably feels kind of remote.

Back to neutral.

Now, *leaders only*, shift your weight forward. Does it feel like into the void, unsupported? Followers feeling a bit crowded? Reverse positions, with leaders in neutral, followers forward. If any of these positions were held for any length of time they would grow very uncomfortable.

And finally, both partners shift your weight **slightly** forward. Isn't that nice? Doesn't it feel good? You're both supporting each other and connecting equally. This forward position is absolutely necessary any time you have your partner in your arms, regardless of whether you are walking backward or forward, or simply standing still. It is through your body that you communicate your movements, and it is not possible to develop a clear lead or follow if you are unable to communicate.

This exercise is a physical experience of what happens emotionally when we communicate. How we either advance or withdraw our emotional positions. If we are not both in a supportive position – say one withdraws from communicating – the other will feel that they are left hanging and resent it, or they are forced to pursue, and resent it. Either way, communication ends, and someone is going to resent it.

The act of communicating requires male and female energy – talking and listening – and to encourage communication and the flow of male and female energy, you must be supportive – or shift forward.

You are now ready to try the Basic Step described in Chapter VIII. His and Her foot diagrams for the Basic Step have been provided as a visual guide, and appear on the next two pages.

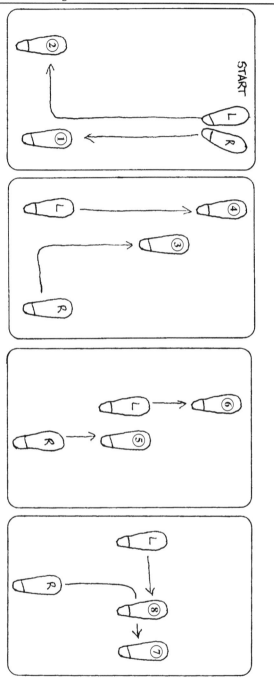

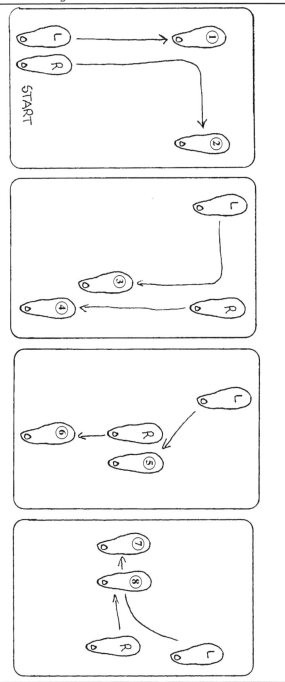

Afterword

Clapping. The act of moving your hands together and apart which creates a sound. Try it. Slowly. Observe your hands as they meet and separate. You are witnessing male and female energy at work. Is one movement better or more powerful than the other? If you think so, stop the movement you think is the weak one and see if you still have clapping. Only together can these two energies create a third thing, in this case, sound.

Consider the notion that "female" energy is weak. It is receptive, while male energy is aggressive. It retreats, while male energy advances.

Now consider throwing a baseball at a net. No matter how hard you throw the ball (male energy) into the net (female energy), it will not bounce back. And the softer the net, the quicker it will stop even the speediest ball. Anyone who has watched a tennis match has witnessed this. So, which is stronger?

Energy in and of itself is not gender specific. It is just energy. But as with anything in the known Universe, it has two sides; and when applied to human energies, these two sides are known as male and female. And while energy propels behavior, it is not, in and of itself, behavior.

Therefore it stands to reason that any modification to the balance of one's energies will ultimately affect one's behavior. And any change in one's own behavior can be reasonably assumed to have some effect, however marginal, on the behavior of others.

This is the concept behind "leading by example". No amount of threatening, cajoling, or promising can make a person change. Allowing people to follow in their own time is a form of surrender; as in Tango, you may lead a step, but you may have to wait before someone follows.

Without understanding female energy (surrender), and embracing it, we will ultimately resort to male energy (control). And, just as in Tango, no one likes to get pushed around.

It would be highly simplistic to think that every problem in the world can be solved by balancing our energies through dance. And yet, as the masters like to remind us, a journey of 1,000 miles begins with the first step. People may change on their own if they perceive change around them, but will do so only in their own time. But until we physically experience both these energies, the fear of one and/or the other will be an obstacle in the path of our balance.

When both men and women we understand the difference between energy and behavior, women will continue to covet male behavior, thinking it will convey them the power men have, and men will do everything in their power to be as different from women as possible since they perceive women as having no power at all.

Developing one energy to the exclusion of the other will and does have detrimental consequences. Without the ability to surrender (female energy), any loss of control (being stuck in traffic, missing the bus, having one's computer crash) produces anger. And everywhere you look, there is anger: road rage, hate crimes, spousal abuse, vandalism.

Without the ability to take control (male energy), we have a hard time making a decision; we feel helpless and depressed, become unmotivated, take drugs, isolate ourselves, and become unproductive.

Unfortunately, our society no longer values the qualities of female energy as highly as those of male energy. As a society we have become overwhelmingly result-oriented, which is masculine, while the process to the result is feminine. We want to know where you went. Which road you took and what you saw along the way is largely irrelevant in our society. But as all travelers know, some of the most interesting things take place "along the way".

Certainly the concept of male and female energy is not original or even new. It is the theme of Ecclesiastes in the Bible (a time to reap a time to sow). And the Chinese made that cool yin/yang symbol centuries before the Anna and Carl Jung wrote Animus/Anima, which is decades before I ever got that fateful phone call.

As for the principles of Tao, although brilliantly described by Benjamin Hoff in The Tao of Pooh, they too have been around much, much longer. It is the basic tenet of this principal – that everything has a natural balance – which I believe perfectly applies to Tango.

But, why Tango? Why not Foxtrot, or the Lambada, or any other ballroom dance? Ballroom dance is structural (behavior). Tango is improvisational (energy). In Ballroom dancing, rhythm determines the connection so close physical is not necessary.

In Tango the exact opposite is true: communication can only be accomplished through a close physical connection. The sole exception may be the rumba, which in any event is much, much simpler, and much more rhythm-driven, a combination which can easily lead to "auto pilot", and thus, diminished "listening".

So Tango, with its infinite variations, requires the woman to completely surrender and follow the lead, and a man to take control and be very clear about his lead. In addition, both partners experience "lead" and "follow" moments throughout each song – in effect switching lead/follow roles. And these energy shifts happen most clearly (for me anyway) in Tango.

In the end though, Tango is only a tool: any change or growth its partnership provokes can only be implemented by the individual. Whatever choices we make – driving drunk, taking drugs, lying, being unfaithful, overeating – we are the only ones ultimately responsible for making them, regardless of any outside pressures, any partners. And true change and growth can only occur when we accept responsibility for our actions.

But accepting responsibility can only be accomplished if your energies are in balance, since "accepting" is female energy. Therefore, the most visible personal consequence of balancing one's energies is accepting responsibility for oneself and one's actions.

Obviously, Tango is not the only place where these energy shifts occur; but for me it's simply the clearest in which to have a physical experience of these opposite energies. Once we become clear about our male and female energies, they can be observed, experienced, and therefore strengthened with ANY activity, including any other partner dance.

Once we understand the difference between energy and behavior, the entire world can become our dance floor.

Letters from Readers

The desire for greater understanding of each other is a universal yearning. It is the reason language was invented. It is also why books, programs, seminars, workshops, and therapies focusing on communication and relationships have never enjoyed more popularity than at present. As our roles change, expand and even merge in our evolving society, there is every-increasing distance between what is said and what is meant. No matter what the situation, men and women will always approach it differently.

Regardless of the type of relationship (professional, personal, familial), its length (first date, childhood friends), or its history (contentious, loving, intellectual), we strive to reconcile, empathize, sympathize, clarify, and debunk. In a world where freedom of expression is enthusiastically encouraged, we are, nonetheless, baffled at our inability to understand each other. Is it then any wonder that we search for the right tools to help us in our efforts?

The tools offered by The Tao of Tango are proving to be very effective, as evidenced by the

following words from people who have worked
with them.

The Tao of Tango is one of the most compelling,
thought-provoking, informative and sensitive books I
have ever read. This book was written from the heart
of the author to the heart of anyone seeking to
understand the interplay of female and male energy in
relationships. The use of the Tango as a metaphor
for the "dance of life" is beautiful and profound in its
simplicity. Your spirit will dance with this one.

Nick Lawrence
Host of "Straight Talk" at weeu.com

...[N]early every sentence you say is a deep and profound truth about tango and real-life-relationships. Your concise language expresses very clearly what I always thought but never formulated in such a lucid way. As a Tanguero and an astrologer (who has written books about relationships in the age of Aquarius)(and as a some-times spiritual healer), I appreciate your insistence on the difference between energy and its expression through behavior.

I' always telling people that Tango is a virtual reality, a simulation of personal relationships, a model of the real thing - but not the real thing itself. Most people confuse emotions created by that sensual dance as its own stage with emotions within a real partnership. But contrary to Shakespeare, the world is not a stage all the time. Or if it is, the plays we perform are rather tragic comedies and we are very bad directors.

Peter R.
PM Magazine

My husband and I attended the Tao of Tango workshop.

When Johanna presents the program she conveys her love for the dance and displays her extraordinary talent when performing the Tango.

Johanna expresses not only her emotions but also the practical applications of the dance, which then makes the understanding of The Tao of Tango clear to all.

We feel that the program is beneficial to couples that have been together for an extended period of time and a good start for couples in the early stages of their relationship. It gives them a chance to explore and communicate their feelings and emotions through not only the beauty of the music but the structure of the dance.

The way we see in which couples benefit from the program are from the teamwork, interaction, respect for themselves, energy of the Tango, and most of all, to trust one another.

We would and have recommended this workshop to other couples.

Roger and Johanna S.

I liked your book quite a bit. I like the way you describe basic Tango movements as metaphors for the way people interact. I also found that the main theme in your writings, including the articles you've written, happens to do with the ways people interact and all of the insecurities associated with that interaction. I do enjoy your writing quite a bit. It has a nice friendly style and your words and flow are well thought out.

My only complaint about The Tao of Tango was that it wasn't long enough! You know that feeling you get when you are reading a book and you're very near the end of the book and you get those mixed feelings of wanting to see how it concludes versus the sense of slight sadness of having completed it? Well, I got that feeling.

John C.
Computers

This book is an excellent primer for anyone whose personal relationships often seem like unarmed conflicts. Although I know almost nothing about Tango; this didn't get in the way of an understanding of the fundamental difference between energy and behavior.

Being male, the concept of female energy residing within me was something I would prefer to not talk about. The Tao of Tango helped me to understand that this energy exists within all of us, and is important in maintaining a balanced, healthy relationship. In fact, I use this energy on a daily basis. This book has made me more aware of this energy, and thus able to use it most effectively. I also have heightened awareness of others' lack of balance in THEIR lives. I would recommend this book to anyone who expects to have lasting, meaningful relationships

Michael S.
Real Estate

The class introduced us to an artful, nuanced
metaphor for the give and take of relationship. Our
30 years together as a couple on the dance floor of
life were laid bare on the dance floor of the Tango for
examination, realignment, and lots of elegant fun.

Toby and Anita C.
Chiropractic

I wanted to let you know how much David and I enjoyed your class, The Tao of Tango. your introductory let us know we'd experience a new way of looking at pairs dancing.

I especially appreciated the stress you placed on the dynamic interplay between the partners. It gave us a great visualization from the moment we embraced and began to move. Also, your demonstrations were inspiring, and I thought the pace of the class was perfect both for novices to learn the basics, and more experienced dancers to savor and experiment with the experience.

Dana P. and David G.
Entertainment Industry

More Praise for
THE TAO OF TANGO
by Johanna Siegmann

"In THE TAO OF TANGO, a fascinating new book by
Johanna Siegmann, readers learn how relationships
are the building blocks of every aspect of their lives."
Book Reviews on Line

"Tango is an art, a physical discipline, and a
philosophy, [and author] Johanna Siegmann has gone
so far as to write a book and create a system of
spiritual training she calls THE TAO OF TANGO."
Kathryn Eastburn, Contributing Editor, Colorado Springs Independent

" THE TAO OF TANGO is excellent! ... I love Ms.
Siegmann's grasp of the essence of femininity and our
need to recognize and submit to it - without
'succumbing'."
Kathryn Blair, Author of *In the Shadow of the Angel*

"[Tango] is an excellent metaphor...to help men and
women get...into a more spiritual union with the
male/female energies that embody each of us. At our
core, we own both and we need to embrace both."
Danny Babineaux, Personal Coach, Miami, FL

"Ms. Siegmann offers us a way to understand the
harmony that exists in the Tango couple and outside
it. To do so she uses ...not only the specific nature of
the Tango relationship, but its general application to

other areas of life...We find pieces of our own lives in
this book...seemingly caught mid-motion."

Historian Gabriel Espinosa, Mexico City, Mexico

THE TAO OF TANGO

For more information,
or to share your
comments, questions, and experiences
with the author
please visit
www.TaoOfTango.com

About the Author

As a consciously curious person, Johanna Siegmann's life-long journey in search of harmony and balance has taken her through many interesting and unusual detours, including crystals, astrology, Tai Chi, Yoga, and mindful meditation.

But it took Tango to change her life.

Born in New York and raised in Mexico, Johanna received a B.A. in English and American Literature from Pitzer College in Claremont, CA. Additional studies included art and theater in England, psychology and philosophy at Cornell, Creative Writing at Hunter College, and playwriting at The New School in New York.

Returning to Mexico after graduation, she began a short-lived career as an advertising copywriter, which eventually brought her back to New York. There, she was bitten by that vicious bug with no known antidote: acting. Writing went backstage.

In the aftermath of a divorce, she came face to face with the Argentine Tango, which turned her life around. It also prompted her to begin writing again.

Johanna has been dancing and performing the Tango since 1995, and has worked as a private coach for several years. Her workshop, based on this book, has been offered by The Learning Annex and has met with great enthusiasm.

In addition to **THE TAO OF TANGO**, Johanna has written three full-length plays, a collection of short-stories, and is currently working on her first novel.

Besides dancing Tango, Johanna writes and directs plays, enjoys hiking in the hills around her home in California, and has a fetish for felines - a trait her darling beloved bravely tolerates.

ISBN 155212410-X

9 781552 124109

Made in the USA
Lexington, KY
11 January 2011